The Book of Common Prayer
Past, Present and Future

The Book of Common Prayer: Past, Present and Future

A 350th Anniversary Celebration

EDITED BY
PRUDENCE DAILEY

continuum

Continuum International Publishing Group
The Tower Building   80 Maiden Lane
11 York Road   Suite 704
London SE1 7NX   New York NY 10038

www.continuumbooks.com

First published 2011
Reprinted 2011, 2012

British Library Cataloguing-in-Publication Data
A catalogue record for this book is available from the British Library.

ISBN: 978-1-4411-2818-8 (paperback)

Extracts from The Book of Common Prayer, the rights in which are
vested in the Crown, are reproduced by permission of the Crown's
Patentee, Cambridge University Press.

Typeset by Fakenham Prepress Solutions, Fakenham,
Norfolk NR21 8NN
Printed and bound in Great Britain

Contents

As Patron of the Prayer Book Society, I am delighted to introduce this anthology, which has been timed to coincide with the forthcoming 350th Anniversary of the 1662 edition of The Book of Common Prayer.

The Prayer Book largely created and spread standard English across the country in the 16th century, when so many people would assemble to hear the cherished and memorable words at Sunday worship in their parish church. Due to the hard work of the Society, the Book remains in use in many churches across the land and has, for hundreds of years, not only enriched our liturgical life, but has also provided a sense of permanence and continuity in an ever-changing landscape.

The vivid and memorable language of The Prayer Book has become part of our Nation's heritage and is, I believe, still vital and necessary to to-day's life. Thomas Cranmer's words were, quite deliberately, like those of Shakespeare, "not of an age but for all time". And so it has survived by passing into common speech. Words and phrases from the liturgy have become part of the heritage of the English language by continuous reiteration through the centuries, in public worship and private devotion. At home and abroad, in hospitals, on battlefields, in solitude, in society, in trouble and in prosperity, these words were remembered and gave comfort and hope in the great crises of innumerable human lives.

And yet, over recent years, we have witnessed a concerted effort to devalue the currency of these resonant words. But who was it who decided that for people who aren't very good at reading, the best things to read are those written by people who aren't very good at writing? Poetry is surely for everybody, even if it's only a few phrases. But banality is for nobody. It might be accessible for all, but so is a desert. It is hard to escape the suspicion that so many changes have been made to the cadence of the language used just to lower the tone, in the belief that the rest of us wouldn't get the point if the word of God was a bit over our heads. But the word of God is supposed to be a bit over our heads…

Perhaps it is worth recalling what George Orwell pointed out in "1984", "that the best way of getting rid of history and thought is to get rid the language of history and ideas."

The essays in this book provide an insight into the history, language and theology of the Book of Common Prayer and so will be of abiding interest not just to those who are already well-versed in its solemn liturgies, but also to those who are keen to learn about a prayer book that has become such a blessing to the faithful of The Church of England and other Anglican churches over so many years.

Section 1

The History of the Book of Common Prayer

A Perusal of the History of the Book of Common Prayer

Neil Patterson

The Revd Neil Patterson is Rector of the Ariconium Benefice in the county and diocese of Hereford. He discovered the Prayer Book concurrently with his faith, at Brasenose College, Oxford. He subsequently trained at Cuddesdon before a curacy in Shropshire. He is Chairman of the Hereford Branch of the Prayer Book Society and served for three years as a Trustee. He is also a parish councillor and Chaplain to Harewood End Agricultural Society. When parish duties permit, he is to be found out on his horse or behind a cricket-scoring table.

Before the Reformation

It is not my intention here to go into the entire history of liturgy until the sixteenth century, nor to enter with any expertise into the various controversies of liturgical history (many of which relate to where or when particular characteristics of the services arose). To understand the Prayer Book it is necessary, however, to have some idea of the liturgical pattern prevailing in England immediately before the Reformation, and which necessarily underlay Cranmer's exertions.

Central to the pre-Reformation Liturgy was the Mass, consisting in practice of a fixed structure and certain unchanging texts, notably the Canon (essentially what is now called the Eucharistic Prayer) and the variable texts for particular feasts and seasons which made up the bulk of the Mass-book, the

Missal. Typical provision for a particular Mass was not only a Collect and Readings, but certain other prayers such as the Secret (used at the offertory) and Psalm verses for Introit, Gradual, Offertory and Communion. For certain days there were more elaborate additions such as the Sequence (before the Gospel) and tropes, i.e. interpolations, in for example the Gloria. Suffice to say that the basic structure and much of the text was close to that of the later Tridentine Mass, but with local variations and a rather more complicated seasonal system. The distinction between Ordinary (invariable) and Proper (seasonal) texts is important, and persists in the Prayer Book (although barely in Common Worship).

The other vital section of liturgy was the daily prayer book of the clergy known as the Breviary, which contained all the necessary material to say the seven daily offices of prayer, assuming the user had the Psalter by heart as was normal. This provided a daily structure of two major offices morning (Matins and Lauds) and evening (Vespers or Evensong and Compline) and three shorter offices through the day (Terce, Sext and None). This structure originated with the Benedictines and had been generally followed, although the form in some religious orders was different and sometimes added a Night Office.

In addition to the two basic books, the medieval Liturgy could also draw on specialized resources for particular ministers or occasions – a Processional with hymns and liturgies for processions, a Pontifical for services proper to the bishop and so on. There were also regional variations – the Uses of Salisbury (Sarum), York, Lincoln, Hereford and Bangor were recognized by Cranmer in his Preface, although on the eve of the Reformation the Sarum Rite was, with the help of the printing press, becoming everywhere dominant.

The entire liturgy was also, of course, in Latin, as it had been since the day St Augustine landed at Thanet nine centuries before. A significant development in the latter Middle Ages, however, had been the Prone, an insertion into the Sunday Mass to allow preaching and some prayer in English. The actual saying (and importantly, singing) of the liturgy (as opposed to attendance) was very much a clerical business – the rubrics of the Sarum Mass in particular make it clear that it was an interaction between the priest at the altar and the clergy in choir, the laity looking on from behind the screen. For educated laity there were many devotional resources available, often referred to as Primers, with appropriate prayers and simplified daily offices.

The Work of Thomas Cranmer

Although the break with Rome is usually dated to the Act of Supremacy of 1534, the later years of Henry VIII's reign saw only mild experiments in liturgical reform, providing some texts in English and making the English Bible available in churches. The birth of the Book of Common Prayer waited until 1549, and the revolution of the First Prayer Book of that year.

The originality of the First Prayer Book cannot be overstated, and the dismissive suggestion of some historians that it was roughly the 'Mass in English' is wholly unsatisfactory. The 1549 Book provided, for the first time ever, the entire worshipping resources (with a Bible) required for a member of the English Church, in English. True, the structure of Holy Communion was close to that at Sarum (albeit much trimmed), and some of the Occasional Offices are closer still. What was swept away, however, was almost the entire elaborate provision for the liturgical year, including such familiar ceremonies as the Ashing, Palms and Easter Liturgy. In their place is a provision of Introits, Collects, Epistles and Gospels for a radically simplified calendar.

The most amazing exercise of all was the reduction of the manifold leaves of the Breviary to a mere ten pages of Matins and Evensong, providing in place of a complicated and clerical office, a simple and strong order that the 'mere ploughboy' could understand, and which could provide a basis for systematic daily reading of the Scriptures. Gone also are the episcopal services, apart from Confirmation and the Ordinal.

Yet it is important to note that unlike most Continental Reformers, Cranmer preserved a liturgical shape to Anglican worship, and to the Christian year. With this combination, of Protestant doctrine and Catholic structure, began the unique vision of the Church of England. Well has it been said that the Prayer Book service of Holy Communion provides the finest *liturgical* expression of the doctrine of salvation by faith alone.

Without spending too long in the byways of Tudor history, it is sufficient to note that there were problems with the First Prayer Book. Continental Reformers, notably Bucer (who had been drafted in as what we would now call a consultant) complained that it was insufficiently radical, and to Cranmer's chagrin the traditionalist Bishop Stephen Gardiner of Winchester professed himself happy to use the Book. The result was the Second Prayer Book of 1552. This took many changes further, cutting out signs of the Cross and ceremonial movement, and breaking up the translated and modified Canon of the Mass to give the familiar 1662 shape of the Holy Communion, with the Prayer of Humble Access and Communion before oblation or thanksgiving. It also saw the introduction of the penitential introduction to Matins and Evensong (now dubbed Morning and Evening Prayer). We are now quite close to 'our' Prayer Book of 1662.

The Prayer Book after Cranmer

The Prayer Book was abolished for the first time by Mary Tudor, who restored the Mass (although allowing the English Litany to remain in use, but no longer seeking deliverance from 'the Bishop of Rome and all his detestable enormities'). In 1559, Elizabeth I restored a form quite close to 1552, although some of the minor amendments are celebrated and significant, for example the Ornaments Rubric, the order to conduct Morning and Evening Prayer in the 'accustomed place' (rather obscurely implying the chancel) and the conflation of the 1549 and 1552 words at the giving of Communion, perhaps the archetypal Anglican compromise by inclusion.

What follows for a century and a half is the remarkable survival of the substance of 1559 through the chaotic struggles of the Stuart dynasty. Throughout the period the Prayer Book stood under attack from the Calvinist or Puritan party, chiefly for retaining various ceremonial elements, and also for using the Apocrypha. Two concessions made were to replace the Epistles and Gospels with the Authorized Version once it had been made, and to augment the prayers after the Anthem in response to a demand for greater intercession. But the 'popish' surplice, wedding ring, funeral service and sign of the cross at baptism were defended again and again, notably at the Hampton Court Conference held shortly after the accession of James I, and the Savoy Conference at the Restoration, which approved the 1662 Book now in force. At the same time, collective Protestant fears of Rome were stoked by the possibility and eventually reality of a Catholic monarch, and no Anglican divine's publications seemed complete without at least a tract against the detestable enormities.

It may be said briefly that although the 1662 settlement remains legally in force, it did not then and has never since commanded the allegiance of all the English. Historians debate the causes of the fall of James II: looked at from a religious perspective, I hope it may be acceptable to state that the Tory Anglicans (i.e. those in favour of the enforcement of the 1662 Prayer Book) turned against their own instincts to ally with the Whigs (either anti-Prayer Book or in favour of toleration) to remove James (Catholic, and therefore ultimately unacceptable to both, whatever their differences). Having made this alliance, there was an abortive attempt in the 1688 Parliament to introduce a 'proto-ASB [Alternative Service Book]' by allowing various options in the Prayer Book to attain universality, but the Tories reverted to form and the Dissenters preferred independence and achieved it legally. Thus ended the history of the Prayer Book as a compulsory liturgy of the realm.

With Dissent permissible and Catholicism no longer actively persecuted, the pressure for change passed, and the Church of England was able to worship content with its own Book. The period was not without controversies (notably over the possible dropping of the Quincunque Vult, otherwise known as the Athanasian Creed), and the life of the Church varied from early puritanical fervour against the first stirrings of modern urban life to the renewal of Wesley and the subsequent Evangelical movement in the early nineteenth century, while many parishes carried on in the loveable slumber depicted in the pages of Parson Woodforde. Through all this, though, the Prayer Book was used happily, and as in every stage of its history, was written about and defended, and the *Rational Illustration* of Wheatley (1710) was a standard work long into the nineteenth century. It may be fair to say that the eighteenth-century Church was self-importantly insular, and that the many references of the period to 'our incomparable Liturgy' were made in relative ignorance of the worship of other churches overseas.

Prayer Books Across the World

As the Church of England began, in not quite coordinated progress with the British Empire, to spread across the globe, it became necessary to find forms for Anglican worship. In many places the 1662 Book was introduced unchanged, and often subsequently translated into local languages, some of which are still in use. I shall not attempt here to consider to what extent they have been amended and replaced in the many autonomous provinces of the Anglican Communion over the last two centuries. It is however, worth recalling the famous adjunct to the seventeenth-century story of the English Prayer Book, the Scottish Book of 1637, introduced unwisely by Laud and Charles I, provoking protest, rebellion, and together with other not insignificant factors, the beheading of them both. The liturgical significance is that the 1637 Book embodied some reversion towards 1549, with the Communion service in a more medieval shape.

Scotland endured its own particular ecclesiastical controversies in the late seventeenth century, culminating in the establishment of Presbyterianism after 1688. Those loyal to the concept of episcopacy were in effect lumped in with the English Non-Jurors (eight bishops and about 400 clergy who resigned their livings rather than break their oath to James II) as illegal schismatics. Given the overall High Church leaning of this group, it was the 1637 Rite that was largely revived by the small group of Episcopalians and formed the basic of the Scottish Rite of 1731. The Non-Jurors divided between those loyal to the Prayer Book and the so-called Usagers, who adopted various interesting liturgical experiments such as the mixed chalice, epiclesis and anointing, but had virtually died out before the subjects arose again in the Oxford Movement.

Apart from Scotland, the 1731 Rite is important because it was exported to the United States when (for political rather than liturgical reasons) the first American bishop, Samuel Seabury, was consecrated by the Scots bishops in 1784. The original American Prayer Book, and its subsequent revisions therefore spring from a different source from others in the Anglican Communion.

Prayer Book Revival
Both the well-known theological movements in the early nineteenth century: the Evangelical Revival and the Oxford Movement, although better known for improving public morality and theological depth respectively, and both for seeking personal sanctity, also brought liturgical consequences within the Church of England. To appreciate this, it is necessary to realize that the normal liturgical practice of an Anglican parish, circa 1800, was of a Sunday service consisting of Matins, Litany and Ante-Communion, followed by a sermon. The service would only continue to the Communion at Christmas, Easter and Whitsun, and then many would leave beforehand (and so the English, with only Easter Communion in the Middle Ages, have *never* been a weekly Eucharistic people). The entire service would normally have been read by the parson, with the clerk making the Responses, and singing limited to metrical psalms around the sermon accompanied

by a band. That at least is the stereotype, confirmed by many sources, although things were very different in choral foundations and doubtless some parishes. It was certainly normal for cathedrals to have a monthly Communion.

The Evangelical push was to encourage congregations to participate in the service, simply in the most basic sense of joining in the appointed Responses and listening to the sermon, rather than reading a book in the security of a box pew or sleeping. When it is put like this, one can see that Wesley had a point. The Evangelicals also began to introduce hymn singing, in imitation of the Methodists, although it was thought radical and emotionalist.

The Oxford Movement took matters a stage further by the simple observation that the Prayer Book provided resources for separate services of Matins, Litany and Communion, and that the Collects, Epistles and Gospels imply the celebration of Communion on *every* Sunday and Feast Day. The Tractarians did not, however, intend to take things beyond the Prayer Book itself: only to do it properly. It is some measure of the conservatism of the combined service that the Shortened Services Act of 1872 had to state directly that Morning Prayer, Litany and Communion could be used as separate services, even though this is quite apparent in the Prayer Book itself.

Whilst the 'advanced' churches pressed on beyond the Prayer Book, as described below, the outworking of the specifically Catholic revival in the Church of England had a profound effect on mainstream worship, sometimes in quite illogical ways. Both liturgy and church architecture came to be in many places dominated by the surpliced choir, seated in prominent stalls and singing large parts of the service whilst the congregation worshipped in silence, whether the weekly worship were Choral Matins or Communion. We are all used to the idea, but forget that the whole concept was newly invented: particularly the prominence of processing in and out singing (cathedral histories remind us that earlier lay clerks were accustomed, monk-like, to potter individually to their places in choir before a service) and the takeover of the anciently clerical chancel by lay musicians.

The services of the Prayer Book also came to be used with a whole array of ceremonial options and all sorts of garments, the history of which almost defies classification (Peter Anson's charming and eccentric 1965, *Fashions in Church Furnishing, 1840–1940*, remains the best attempt), and it will not be done here. But relics of musty controversies over surplice length and dalmatic drape linger still in certain quarters.

Prayer Book Amendment (failed)

The combination of Roman Catholic emancipation, easier continental travel for middle-class clergymen and the activities of briefly fashionable sects like the Irvingites awakened Victorian Anglicans to the breadth of Christian tradition hitherto much unregarded by their insular forefathers. With a suddenness which in retrospect appears extraordinary, many clergy, perhaps first of all Hurrell Froude, took up the position to be found throughout Anglo-Catholic history, that, although it fortunately preserved the gist of Catholic Christianity, the Prayer Book of the Church of England was a basically inadequate resource for expressing this, and needed to be supplemented by many direct textual and ceremonial borrowings from the Roman Missal.

Most of the history of the period follows the course of the notable legal cases, which in turn were more concerned with ceremonial (i.e. vestimentary and decorative) controversies than ritual (variation of words); and in both there were many variations and divergences, of which the bitter divide between Roman (i.e. looking to contemporary Europe) and Sarum (i.e. looking to the English Middle Ages) was only the most prominent. Right at the end of the period the English Liturgy movement, expressed through the Alcuin Club, emerged with the distinct aim of ceremonial revival within the Prayer Book, but it was much too late to stem the tide of disorder.

A Royal Commission on Public Worship of 1906 set in train the slow process of liturgical revision, although work on different revised liturgies did not begin in earnest until after the hiatus of the Great War. The war also brought to prominence the particularly controversial question of Prayer for the Dead. In the great national grief various ambiguous forms of prayer were authorized, but the Anglo-Catholic movement found great appeal in the theme of the communion of living and departed across the altar. Different factions proposed varying amendments to the Prayer Book, with particular focus on the Holy Communion service, where greater accessibility to ancient texts had made liturgical scholars aware of the historical eccentricity of Cranmer's arrangement.

The proposed Prayer Book was debated by the Church Assembly in 1927, and again in slightly amended form in 1928. In both years, however, it was defeated in the House of Commons by an expedient political alliance of strong Protestants (organized by the still-flourishing Church Society) who feared any change towards the Mass (which could be a rather hysterical description of the 1928 Book) and Anglo-Catholics who were enjoying illegal freedom and feared enforced conformity to a mildly revised Prayer Book that was supposed to accommodate them (some Anglo-Catholic sisterhoods held all-night vigils against the 1928 Book through the parliamentary sittings). This defeat was of considerable importance in the history of the Established Church, as it signalled the last significant Parliamentary Act in English Church history, and the point at which many churchmen came to believe that an independent authority for the Church was needed, something it took until 1970 fully to achieve in the form of General Synod. It is worth noting that almost nothing of the 1662 Prayer Book was to be lost under the 1928 proposals, but all new material introduced as alternative or supplementary, with the supplementary services placed in an appendix. It is also notable that all the material was written in mock-Tudor English of varying quality, and therefore sits readily with the 1662 services. A few 1928 texts (the alternative introduction to Matins and Evensong, additional sentences of Scripture, the shorter Commandments) have survived into contemporary use in many places, partly through inclusion in the small green Shorter Prayer Book published in 1946 and still available. The painstakingly revised Prayer of Consecration (with in fact so few words different from 1662) has on the other hand been consigned to history.

Prayer Book Replacement

Neither the mood of the 1950s nor the personality of Archbishop Fisher, were conducive to further official liturgical experiment, and it was not until the 1960s that change began again. By this time, world Christianity had been transformed by ecumenical progress and the Second Vatican Council, and liturgy by the emergence of the Pauline Missal and its translation into contemporary English and other languages. There is little need here to detail the progress of congregations through the Series 1, 2 and 3 Rites towards the ASB, particularly for readers who remember the whole process well, as I do not. For those who do not remember, the Communion services in particular in Series 1, 2, 3 correspond roughly to 1928, and ASB Rites B and A respectively. More significant is that under the guidance of Dean Jasper, the Liturgical Commission proceeded to design the new services as alternatives to the Prayer Book, avoiding both the legal and political difficulty of repealing the 1662 Act of Uniformity, and somewhat blunting the challenge of the newly founded Prayer Book Society.

What came into being for universal use was the ASB of 1980, offering completely revised services in modern, arguably rather bland, English. Looking back, the ASB is striking for the limited range of services provided, all alternatives to the main Prayer Book rites. Anglican worship has since then been complicated by the introduction of supplementary seasonal services, beginning with *Lent, Holy Week and Easter,* in 1984 and *The Promise of His Glory* in 1990, which as additional material require only the commendation of the House of Bishops rather than resolution of General Synod.

All these services, with little amendment, and many more, are now authorized and published in the veritable library of

Common Worship and presented in a form comparatively easy to understand, copy and amend. It is notable, however, that Common Worship proclaims an intention to constrain Anglican worship within broad limits, of keeping up some degree of liturgical structure (as expressed in a Service of the Word), more so for Holy Communion, and not authorizing texts widely used by Anglo-Catholics that make explicit their adoption of Eucharistic or hagiological doctrines not acceptable to Anglicans at large.

Alongside all this the Book of Common Prayer [BCP] of 1662 remains inviolate, the only Liturgy specifically legalized by Act of Parliament. This normativity was brought home to those PCCs [Parochial Church Councils] who were told rightly in 2000 that if they did not vote to use the alternative of Common Worship, the abolition of the ASB left them with the Prayer Book as the only legal option. Practical reality on the ground varies widely, although the modern Common Worship Eucharist is almost certainly the most common service across the parishes of England, but it is also probably fair to say that almost every form of service invented from 1662 until today is still in use somewhere, maybe closer than you think.

English Society, Religion and the Book of Common Prayer

Raymond Chapman

Professor the Revd Raymond Chapman is Emeritus Professor of English in the University of London and a non-stipendiary priest in the Diocese of Southwark. He is a Vice-President of the Prayer Book Society and of the Anglican Association and is a Fellow of the English Association. He has published a number of books on academic and devotional subjects and has frequently contributed to Faith and Worship *and the* Prayer Book Society Journal. *His recent books include edited selections from the works of Richard Hooker and Lancelot Andrewes.*

The story of the Book of Common Prayer is not an isolated archive separated from the mainstream of English history. It is a record of social and political as well as religious changes. The revisions which have been made to it, both major and minor, have not been the whims of liturgists; they were occasioned by changes in the Church, which in themselves were responding to pressures from the wider community.

The first Book of Common Prayer was compiled after major religious upheavals in England. The Reformation had been in progress for over 30 years, with its roots reaching back long before Luther nailed his theses to the church door in Wittenberg. The demand for the Bible and services to be in the vernacular instead of Latin had spread across Europe. England was comparatively late in responding. An English

15

Litany printed in 1544 (as an act of corporate prayer which it was hoped would assist the nation in its current war against France), was the first such service to be authorized, although there had already been some tentative use of vernacular passages within the Mass.

The factors at work here are well known. There was the influx of Protestant ideas from continental scholars, or from English ones who had studied abroad. Politically there was the 'King's matter': the attempt of Henry VIII to get an annulment of his marriage to Catherine of Aragon; his fury at the Pope's refusal to grant it; his repudiation of papal supremacy; his new title as Supreme Head of the Church in England and the redirection to the royal treasury of payments previously sent to Rome. If the Church of England thus redefined was to establish itself as a true but independent part of the Holy, Catholic and Apostolic Church, it needed to determine its doctrine and its liturgy.

This was the task of Thomas Cranmer, Archbishop of Canterbury. Following his meeting with other bishops at Chertsey Abbey, the first Book of Common Prayer was issued in 1549 with the injunction that it was to be used in all churches in the realm. It contained all that was needed in the worship of the Church: daily office services, the Holy Communion and services for the great occasions of individual lives. It was also, and has continued to be, its own instruction manual. The rubrics are many and precise, a complete guide to clergy confronted with new services. Further rubrics including how to deal with the irregular number of Sundays after Trinity in different years and the procedure when the conse-crated bread and wine prove to be insufficient, were added in 1662.

It was influenced by previous service books, notably the Sarum Rite. It kept some Catholic emphases, such as the continuation of the Prayer of Consecration by a prayer of oblation while the consecrated elements were still on the altar. But it was clearly not just the Roman Rite in English. The Eucharist was now called 'The Supper of the Lord and the Holy Communion', with the word 'Mass' relegated to 'Commonly called the Mass'. More frequent lay worship and more lay participation were encouraged, and made easier by the use of English. The liturgical work of the clergy was simplified by having everything in one book, as the Preface proudly declared.

While historians are in general agreement about what happened, they differ about how it was received by the country as a whole. Roman Catholic writers may see the English Reformation as something thrust by power upon an unwilling populace, which remained secretly loyal to Rome. Others claim that for the majority the new order was a liberation, the religious expression of the growing pride in English nationalism. The voice of the people is always hard to determine. The voice of power is more fully recorded, and in this instance it is not a single voice. The nobles who had profited from the dissolution of the monasteries were well pleased with their new wealth and supported the clerical authorities who welcomed the new order. There was also a faction at Court which was not happy about the changes and was hoping for a reversal. The first Prayer Book was generally accepted by the people of the land, no doubt then as now with a few grumbles about any innovation in services. There was a more serious protest in the West Country, with a rising of those who insisted that the old order should be restored. They declared that 'We will not have the new service, because it is but like a Christmas game; but we will have our old service of Matins, Mass, Evensong and procession in Latin not in English'.

On the other hand, the Book of 1549 was too conservative for some of the more extreme Reformers and there was pressure on Cranmer to produce a revised version. The precocious boy Edward VI was in favour of Reformed worship, as were the two successive Protectors during his minority, the Dukes of Somerset and Northumberland. Influenced by Continental Reformers like Bucer and Peter Martyr, and guided also by his own increasingly Reformed thinking, Cranmer brought the Second Prayer Book into the Church in

1552. It was distinctly more Protestant in tone. The Prayer of
Consecration in the Communion service now ended abruptly
with the Words of Institution, proceeding immediately to the
Communion of the people, and the original continuation
became one of two post-Communion prayers.

The Second Prayer Book had less than a year of life. When
Edward VI died in 1553, he was succeeded by his half-sister
Mary (daughter of Catherine of Aragon), who had kept her
Roman obedience. She quickly brought the country back to
allegiance to the Pope, the Prayer Book was suppressed and
the Roman Mass restored. The sad story of her reign is well
known: years when the martyrdom of determined Protestants
left a wound between Canterbury and Rome, which took long
to heal. The damage was made worse by the martyrdom of
Roman Catholic priests and laity in the next reign.

Elizabeth I, who succeeded in 1558, was the daughter of
Anne Boleyn, inheriting a Reformed tradition to which she
had held firm, sometimes at personal peril, in the previous
reign. The Church of England had not yet established its
identity. In little more than two decades, centuries of papal
supremacy had been broken, the king declared Supreme Head
of the Church in his realm, advanced Reformed worship introduced, and all swept away by a return to Rome. The people of
England were bruised by continual change, some hoping for a
return to stronger Reformation principles, some for continuation of papal authority, the majority bewildered and longing
for peace and assurance.

This was the inheritance of Elizabeth as a young woman
of 25. In 1558, the questions were many and urgent. Under
whose authority would the Church of England be governed?
Would its structure still be episcopal? In what form, and in
what language, would public worship be conducted? Elizabeth
was intelligent, well informed and less intransigent than her
late brother and sister. She was personally devout, distrustful
of the extremes which had been tearing the country apart,
tolerant by nature but aware of the need for firm central
control. In worship, her preference was for a moderate

Catholic practice. There were lights and a crucifix on the altar in her private chapel but she forbade elevation of the Host and rebuffed the monks of Westminster who greeted her with candles, saying 'Away with those torches, for we see very well'. Here was a ruler who many hoped could bring stability and a peaceful settlement for the religion of the nation.

The Book of Common Prayer, splendid in language and precise in formulation, was ready for renewed authority: but which Book – conservative 1549 or radical 1552? In January 1559, Elizabeth's first Parliament passed two Acts which set the course for the restored Church. The Act of Supremacy affirmed that neither the Pope nor any foreign power had jurisdiction in England, and declared that the Queen was 'Supreme Governor' in all matters both of Church and State. It was a small but subtle difference from the title of 'Supreme Head' taken by Henry VIII. The Act of Uniformity required the use in all public worship of the Book of Common Prayer. It was effectively the 1552 version; Elizabeth, and many others favoured the 1549 Book, but there was enough pressure for the opinion of some of the more extreme Reformers to prevail.

The 1559 Book contained several changes, notably the omission of the petition in the Litany to be delivered from 'the Bishop of Rome and all his detestable enormities'. More important doctrinally was the change in the words of administration at Holy Communion, showing that spirit of inclusion, which has always been a mark of Anglicanism. In 1549, the bread was given with the words 'The body of our Lord Jesus Christ which was given for thee preserve thy body and soul unto everlasting life', the cup similarly with 'The blood of our Lord Jesus Christ which was shed for thee ...' The form was changed in 1552 to 'Take and eat this in remembrance that Christ died for thee, and feed on him in thy heart by faith with thanksgiving', and 'Drink this in remembrance that Christ's blood was shed for thee, and be thankful'. The first formula affirmed the Real Presence; the replacement gave the signal that the Eucharist was a memorial, an act of obedience to the dominical command rather than a sacramental sharing. It accommodated the receptionist view of some Reformers that grace received in Communion came through the faith of the communicant and not through any change in the elements. The Elizabethan Prayer Book put the two forms together, as they have remained to this day, acceptable to all consciences. The word 'and' was printed between the 1549 and 1552 words, whether as a reminder to the priest or to emphasize both interpretations to the communicant is uncertain; the word was removed in 1662.

Another move away from strict Reformed principles in the 1559 Book, was the omission of the words added at the end of the Holy Communion service in 1552, explaining that the rule of kneeling to receive Communion was intended to keep due order and reverence, but that 'it is not meant thereby that any adoration is done, or ought to be done, either unto the Sacramental bread or wine there bodily received or to any real and essential presence there being of Christ's natural body and blood'. Known as the Black Rubric – not for any critical reason but because it was printed in black instead of the usual red for rubrics – its excision took away any absolute bar to accepting the Real Presence.

Less doctrinal but the source of much controversy was the 'Ornaments Rubric' printed before the Order for Morning Prayer. It ordered that the minister 'shall use such ornaments in the church as were in use by the authority of Parliament in the second year of the reign of King Edward the VI, according to the Act of Parliament set in the beginning of this book'. With its reference to 1549, the year of the first and more Catholic Prayer Book, it was probably intended as a conservative provision, but in practice there was a reaction against ornaments and vestments, even the surplice being regarded by some as popish. The rubric was retained, with a slight change of wording, in 1662. During the ritualist controversies in the nineteenth century it was appealed to both by supporters and opponents of Eucharistic vestments. Prayers for the Queen and for the clergy and people were added after the Litany and are still printed after the orders for Morning and Evening

Prayer. In the Lectionary, proper Old Testament Lessons were provided for every Sunday in the year.

The Act of Uniformity was supported by a list of Royal Injunctions, setting out rules for clerical dress, bowing and kneeling at appropriate times, ordering the clergy to be more attentive to preaching and catechising, and prohibiting any man in holy orders from marrying without the approval of his bishop. There was enough in the Prayer Book and the Injunctions to rouse opposition among those who had hoped for a more strongly Reformed settlement, and the seeds of decades of controversy were sown. The long reign of Elizabeth I saw objections by the more advanced Protestants, who pressed for less structured worship and for the centrality of the sermon rather than the sacrament. There was also a continual threat from plots made by those loyal to the Pope, encouraged by the excommunication of the Queen in 1570. In 1562 John Jewel, Bishop of Salisbury, published a vigorous defence of the Anglican settlement. His *Apologia Ecclesiae Anglicanae* claimed that reform of the Church had been essential, that the newly formed Council of Trent could not serve the purpose, and that national churches had the right to pass their own legislation through provincial synods. The other principal apologist for the Church of England was Richard Hooker in his *Lawes of Ecclesiastical Politie*, particularly aimed at the Puritan opposition and with a scholarly and reasoned defence of the Prayer Book in the fifth volume.

In spite of the controversies and acts of disobedience, the Elizabethan Settlement was carried through peacefully as compared with wars of religion elsewhere in Europe. Public services other than those in the Prayer Book were illegal, but generally there was not any close enquiry into details of usage, unless complaint was made or there was extreme deviation. There was no compromise on the assumption that Church and State were linked together. There was no place for a theocracy or any independent authority.

The accession of James I in 1603 brought hope both to the Roman Catholic minority, because of the faith of his mother Mary Queen of Scots; and also, to the more advanced Reformers, because he came from the Presbyterian Scotland of John Knox. In the event, James supported the Established Church and was a strong defender of episcopacy as inseparable from monarchy. Nevertheless, the Puritan opponents were beginning to feel their strength and presented a petition for certain changes to be made. In reply, the Hampton Court Conference was convened in 1604: it heard, but did not accede to, Puritan demands for such changes as the abolition of the sign of the Cross in baptism and bowing at the Name of Jesus, and use of words such as 'priest' and 'absolution' which were considered to have popish associations. Concessions were few and minor, such as adding 'or remission of sins' to the title 'Absolution', prayers for the Royal Family as well as the king, and some prayers for specific Thanksgivings. The chief and glorious outcome of the conference was the Authorized or King James Version of the Bible in 1611.

James kept the religious opposition at bay. The reign of his son Charles I saw a movement back to attitudes and practices which would later be considered 'High Church' but which then were seen by some as a reversion towards Rome. Charles approved and encouraged the work of William Laud, Archbishop of Canterbury and other like-minded divines. These were the outward signs of a short but confident period of Anglican worship, grounded in the Book of Common Prayer. More important was the doctrinal work of the Caroline divines, as they are often known, which consolidated and took forward the work of Jewel and Hooker. They looked to the early Church, going back before the medieval developments which were defended by the Roman Church and denigrated by the Puritans, promoting a middle way which would be not a mere compromise but a positive assertion of the place of the Church of England in the Universal Church. William Laud was a powerful writer as well as a vigorous archbishop. Lancelot Andrewes, Bishop successively of Chichester, Ely and Winchester, and one of the principal translators of the Authorized Version, preached often before the king and left to posterity a set of prayers which are rich in the pursuit of holiness. Henry Hammond wrote a *Practical Catechism* to expound and make accessible Church teaching. George Herbert wrote the finest set of poems inspired by membership of the Church of England and also a prose work, *A Priest to the Temple*, which reflects his own devotion and gives advice which is still relevant to ordained ministry. Nicholas Ferrar established a small community at Little Gidding in Huntingdonshire where he, with his family and others, kept a rule of regular devotion based on the Book of Common Prayer.

The causes of the Civil War, which began in 1642, were not only religious, but the conflict generally aligned Anglicans against Puritan Parliamentary supporters, including several small and extreme sects as well as the more orthodox Presbyterians and Independents. The community at Little Gidding was destroyed in 1646. Both Charles and Laud were executed and, in spite of their faults, many still regard them as Anglican martyrs.

As the Parliamentary forces became more powerful and eventually victorious, it could have seemed that the Book of Common Prayer was gone for ever. Its use was forbidden in 1645, at first in public worship and then even for private devotion, and all copies were to be surrendered. The new governing power issued a 'Directory for Public Worship'. This was not a prayer book, but a book of instructions for the conduct of services. Predictably, it forbade all the Anglican practices to which the Puritans had previously objected, and gave prominence to the sermon. There was no direction for a Burial Service: interment was specifically to be done 'without ceremony'. Holy days and festivals, including Christmas, were abolished. The diarist John Evelyn recorded how Cromwellian soldiers interrupted a service and threatened the congregation on Christmas Day 1657.

The rule of Oliver Cromwell as Lord Protector, known as the Commonwealth, ended with his death in 1659. In May of the following year, the monarchy was restored in the person of Charles II, and the Church of England was re-established. The Prayer Book was restored to its rightful place, but it was time for a new look at its contents. The people were weary and bewildered by change and innovation, as they had been when Elizabeth I came to the throne. But not all that had happened since 1642 could be ignored. The Presbyterian presence was still strong, and Church leaders were not generally committed to the Laudian approach.

The Savoy Conference met in the following year, a joint meeting of Anglicans wanting to establish a revised but firm liturgical order and Presbyterians not totally opposed to the Prayer Book but demanding a number of changes. The result of long and sometimes heated discussion was the 1662 Book of Common Prayer. Among the additional services, an important innovation was the Order for Adult Baptism, introduced mainly to give a way of rectifying some of the irregularities of the previous decade, and also for the purpose, less agreeable to a post-imperialist world, of 'baptising natives in our plantations'. The wonderful General Thanksgiving was written by Bishop Edward Reynolds. The Presbyterian objection to the Benedicite as an alternative to the Te Deum at Morning Prayer, on the ground that it was from the Apocrypha, was not upheld. However, by Presbyterian desire, the Epistles and Gospels were now printed according to the Authorized Version. Most other Scripture passages, including the Psalter appended to the main Book, remained as in the earlier translation. Differences can be seen, for example, in the Ten Commandments and the Comfortable Words.

Some more specifically Catholic emphases appeared. The rubric for the manual acts at Communion, included in 1549 but omitted in 1552, was restored. The Absolution at Matins and Evensong was now to be said specifically by the 'Priest', not the 'Minister'. The 'Black Rubric' removed in 1559, was restored, with a slight but significant change of wording. The 1552 version rejected adoration of 'Any *real and essential* presence there being of Christ's natural flesh and blood'. The 1662 rubric has 'Any *corporal* presence of Christ's natural flesh and blood' (italics added). This continues to reject the subtle philosophy of transubstantiation but gives a more open way to belief in the Real Presence. What emerged from the Savoy Conference was essentially the 1552 Book enriched by additions and with more honouring of the earlier tradition. The new Preface explained the changes, beginning with the very Anglican declaration, 'It hath been the wisdom of the Church of England, ever since the first compiling of her Publick Liturgy, to keep the mean between the two extremes, of too much stiffness in refusing, and of too much easiness in admitting, any variation from it'.

The royalist and Anglican euphoria of the Restoration moderated in the next two decades. When Charles II died in 1685, he was succeeded by his brother James, a convert to Roman Catholicism, which since the sad reign of Mary had been regarded with hostility by the majority of English people. The revolution of 1688 brought the expulsion of James and his new-born son, later to be known as the Old Pretender. The Protestant William of Orange, husband of James's daughter by his first marriage, was invited to take the throne and to reign jointly with his wife.

The Presbyterian and other Dissenters had not given up hope that their demands for change in the Prayer Book might be met. There had been attempts to improve the position of those who would not conform to the usage of the Established Church, and were suffering severe restrictions on their personal freedom. These did not succeed, but the new king came in on a wave of Protestant enthusiasm. William promised to find a way to 'a good agreement between the Church of England and Protestant Dissenters'. (There was no sympathy for Roman Catholics.) Again there was no formal legislation but in practice a slight degree of tolerance was granted.

Parliament asked for a meeting of the Convocation of the Clergy, which had been in abeyance for many years. Convocation met in 1689, to consider revision of the Liturgy and Canons as a way to reconciliation. There was a formidable list of demands, many restated from those refused by

the Savoy Conference. In the rubrics, 'priest' was to revert
to 'minister' and 'Lord's Day' substituted for 'Sunday'. There
was no possibility that the many and often tendentious
demands would be passed by the Lower House of clergy,
although the bishops generally were in favour of some concessions. Eventually Convocation was prorogued without formal
consideration of the document and was not convened again
until 1852.

The eighteenth century brought no revisions of the Prayer
Book, which, despite the opposition of Dissenters, had established itself in the affection of the majority of English people.
It continued to enrich both literature and common speech
with its language, as well as preserving the doctrinal basis of
the Established Church. But in what may seem to have been a
peaceful and even complacent period in ecclesiastical history,
there was diversity of liturgical opinion. The Non-Jurors,
successors of clergy ejected for refusing to take the Oath of
Allegiance to William III, at first worshipped with the 1662
Book but later produced more than one liturgy of their
own, largely derived from 1549 and taking a more Catholic
position. There were various agitations, some carried on
through polemical pamphlets, for further revisions. These were
often, though not exclusively, made by holders of views which
tended to a Unitarian position and disliked the firm Trinitarian
doctrine of the Prayer Book. In the absence of Convocation,
and with a general weariness of theological controversy and a
desire for stability, no proceedings were taken.

However, the climate of opinion was changing. Acts of
relief for Protestant Dissenters in 1828 and Roman Catholics
in 1829 showed the beginning of a more tolerant spirit and a
more confident churchmanship, though true ecumenism was
far in the future. One sign of a more comprehensive view
came in 1859 with removal from the Prayer Book of the State
Services which had been added in the seventeenth century.
The failure of the 1605 'Gunpowder Plot' was celebrated on 5
November in a service which included some very intemperate
language about the Roman Catholic Church. The execution

of Charles I was commemorated on 30 January and the Restoration of the monarchy in 1660 on 29 May. These were annexed by royal warrant and not an integral part of the 1662 book, and were removed by royal warrant in 1859. Less antagonism to Rome, and perhaps a feeling that a celebration of the Stuart dynasty was not wholly appropriate for a monarchy in the Hanoverian succession, may have been influential. The service for the yearly anniversary of the accession of the sovereign remained and has been revised in each new reign. It is a coincidence, but a perhaps a significant one, that these liberal changes were made in the same year as Darwin's *Origin of Species* and the year before *Essays and Reviews* by seven Anglican writers influenced by the new biblical criticism, which caused much opposition within the Church.

A Commission of Inquiry into the conduct of public worship did not reach agreement on the question of ritual practised by clergy influenced by the Oxford Movement, a controversy which led to the Public Worship Regulation Act in 1874. However, the third report of the Commission in 1871 brought a radical revision of the Lectionary for Morning and Evening Prayer. It also led to the Shortened Services Act in 1872. This allowed Matins and Evensong to begin with 'O Lord, open thou our lips', omitting the Confession. The Act also permitted various reductions such as the use of one canticle at Matins and Evensong, and the saying of fewer Psalms. It made no difference to the full use of the 1662 Book, but was a recognition that the daily offices were in many places becoming truly daily instead of only on Sundays.

Since that time, the use of the Book of Common Prayer has continued, with increasing tolerance for different applications and interpretations, as the Church of England became more comprehensive and also more ecumenical. The last attempt at a major revision, as distinct from its replacement, began in 1904 when a Royal Commission decided that 'the law of public worship in the Church of England is too narrow for the religious life of the present generation'. Any action was postponed by the Great War, but in 1927 proposals for revisions and additions to the Book of Common Prayer came before Parliament. They were defeated then, and again in the following year, mainly through strong Protestant opposition in the Commons to such matters as Prayer for the Dead and a cautious provision for Reservation. There were also objections to the Alternative Order for Holy Communion, allowing the Gloria at the beginning of the service and the continuation of the Prayer of Consecration as in 1549. Although it was never authorized, the bishops generally accepted it tolerantly and much that the 1928 Book offered was widely adopted. More Propers for saints' days, additional prefaces, and modifications to the marriage and funeral services, have been acceptable to many. The shortening of the Venite, to omit the final more admonitory verses, was perhaps not quite such a good idea. It was a foretaste of the retreat from acknowledging the severe obligations as well as the benefits of faith which is too prevalent today. Opinions about 1928 still differ, but it is a useful Book containing all that is in 1662, requiring nothing more, but offering some additions in traditional language.

What came later is well known. The *Alternative Service Book* in 1980 was received with enthusiasm by many clergy and led to some denigration of the Book of Common Prayer. The issue of *Common Worship* in 2000 offered a wider choice of services and came into use more peacefully. Its Preface declares that 'The Book of Common Prayer remains the permanently authorized provision for public worship in the Church of England, whereas the newer liturgies are authorized until further resolution of the General Synod'.

Over four and a half centuries, the fortunes of the Book of Common Prayer have both reflected and sustained the evolution of the Church of England. Catholic and Protestant emphases have been brought into harmony, within the famous *via media*, which is still a concept not to be despised. Cautious addition and conservative revision have recognized changes in society and religious thinking. The Evangelical Revival and the Oxford Movement both revitalized the Church, called it back to neglected truths, and found their expression in the same liturgy. There are surely few today who would oppose all liturgical change or doubt the integrity and scholarship of those who compile new services. But wisdom and discretion will continue to acknowledge the centrality of the Book of Common Prayer. The Church of England is not built on a foundation document like the Westminster Confession, or a central authority like the Roman *magisterium*. It remains tolerant and comprehensive, but it has a written source to affirm and preserve its distinctive identity. It may be likened to the man of whom our Lord speaks, bringing forth from his treasure things both new and old.

From Cranmer to Bancroft: The Origin of the Book of Common Prayer 1549–1604

David Loades

*After completing his PhD at Cambridge in 1961 under Sir Geoffrey Elton, **Professor David Loades** taught successively at the Universities of St. Andrews (1961–63), Durham (1963–80) and Wales, Bangor where he held the Chair of History from 1980 to 1995. He is now an honorary member of the History Faculty of the University of Oxford. From 1993 to 2004, he was Director of the British Academy John Foxe Project, producing an on-line edition of the Acts and Monuments and printed works under his editorship. In 2005, he edited a collection of essays on the Book of Common Prayer entitled* Word and Worship *(Davenant Press). He has written extensively on the English Reformation most recently* The Religious Culture of Marian England *(Ashgate, 2010).*

The medieval Church of England made use of many liturgical works, derived mostly (but not exclusively) from the Roman Rite. These included Processionals, Psalters and Legends, but the commonest were the Missal and the Primer. The first of these contained the Ordinary, Canon, Collects, and various other parts of the Mass in all its varied forms, and the latter, also known as the *Horae*, contained the Hours of the Blessed Virgin and a variety of other prayers. All these books were written in Latin, and were intended for use by the clergy. At a time when the vast majority of the laity were illiterate, there was little objection to this. The most generally used set was that derived from the practice of Salisbury Cathedral and was known as the Sarum Use, although other uses, derived from Hereford and York also had a local currency. In the early sixteenth century the demands for reform of the Church arose largely from the increasing literacy of the lay community, particularly in the towns, and one of the first things that Martin Luther did was to produce a 'Kirchen-Ordnungen', or scheme of services in the vernacular. He also, of course, translated the New Testament into German. In order to meet this demand for reform without lapsing into heresy, Clement VII commissioned Cardinal Quiñones to produce a new Breviary, restoring the 'ancient simplicity' of the rites, and this was published in 1535. This was in Latin and was reasonably successful, but was withdrawn in the early days of the Counter Reformation, in 1558. Then in 1542, Herman von Wied, the archbishop of Cologne, attempted to bridge the gap between Catholics and Lutherans by publishing an orthodox Church order written in the vernacular and based partly on the work of the Strasburg Reformer Martin Bucer. However, this was deemed to be too heretical and von Wied was excommunicated and his work banned in 1546.

The English Church, as constituted under Henry VIII, was well placed to meet a similar challenge. Doctrinally orthodox, but jurisdictionally independent, and not bound by rules or opinions emanating from Rome, in December 1534, Convocation petitioned the king for an authorized translation of the Scriptures. Henry responded by approving the Coverdale version in October 1535, and this opened the way to experiments with an English Liturgy. In 1542, a new edition of the Sarum Breviary was prepared, bearing clear signs of the Royal Supremacy, and in the following year provision was made for the New and Old Testament readings to be in English. In 1544 'certayne godly prayers and suffrages' were also set forth in English, and the Litany was translated. Then in 1545 appeared King Henry's primer in both Latin and English, specifically for that (now fairly large) constituency which was literate in the latter but not in the former. The laity was thus fairly well accustomed to praying in English by the time of Henry's death in January 1547. This resulted in a change of regime which opened the way for the introduction of Protestantism, a development which the old king had always resisted. The first sign of what was coming was the issue, in the summer of 1547, of Archbishop Cranmer's *Book of Homilies*. For the first time laymen had a chance to read scriptural exposition which was independent of the opinions of their parish priest, and although preaching was urged upon the clergy as a solemn duty, it was an obligation more honoured in the breach than in the observance. Many laymen relied for their enlightenment mainly on the *Homilies*. At the beginning of 1548, questions were submitted to the bishops about the desirability of translating the whole liturgy into English, and serious reservations were expressed, particularly over the Canon of the Mass, which conservatives considered to embody a sacred mystery. This changed the whole nature of the debate, because hitherto it had been about custom and utility, but now it was over the doctrine of transubstantiation. This, Protestants rejected on the grounds that it was both unreasonable and unscriptural. Nevertheless a compromise was reached on 8 March 1548 whereby the Canon was issued in English, but without any change in the traditional teaching. Significantly called *The Order of Communion*, it implied a shift of emphasis from the consecration to reception, but did not explicitly reject transubstantiation. Moreover, although it was enjoined, it was not imposed. The order was inevitably controversial, but the controversy was damped down on 24 April, when all preaching on the subject was forbidden by proclamation.

Cranmer and his Protestant allies were not satisfied. The archbishop had abandoned transubstantiation at some point in 1548, and wanted an order which reflected his current convictions. In September 1548 a committee of bishops and other divines was established to prepare 'a uniform order of prayer', and almost certainly considered a draft which Cranmer had already written, because its work was complete by 15 December, when a debate was launched on the subject in Parliament. The debate was doctrinal, but it was clearly about the 'uniform order', which appears to have been modified somewhat in the process. It was then attached as an annexe to the Act of Uniformity which was going through Parliament at the same time, and carried in both Houses by 21 January. It was not, apparently, submitted to either Convocation, but nevertheless became legally binding when the session ended on 14 March. Whitsunday, 9 June, was the date fixed for its implementation. Fundamentally this first Book of Common Prayer was a translation of those parts of the Sarum Use which were deemed to be most appropriate, including Morning and Evening Prayer, and the rites of baptism, marriage and burial. It included parts of the Greek Rite, and of the Order of Herman von Wied. Its most important innovation, however, which was truly revolutionary, was the replacement of the traditional Mass with a Communion service. The wording of the Canon was only slightly altered, but the rubrics both forbade the elevation of the Host, which was central to the ancient rite, and required members of the congregation to Communicate with the priest. The elements were now deemed to be imbued with the spiritual presence of Christ, but not with that corporeal presence which had been the essence of the traditional order. The whole symbolism of the service was thus changed from being an act of sacrifice, performed by the priest for the benefit of the people, into a solemn commemorative meal in which the whole congregation was invited to take part. The 'miracle of the Mass' thus disappeared, and with it the fundamental underpinning of sacerdotal authority. The celebrant of the 1549 Communion

was still called a priest, but his function was now that of
a minister.[1]

The object of the Book of Common Prayer was not only to
shift the doctrinal basis of the Church into a moderate form of
Protestantism, but also to provide a uniform order of service
for the whole Church, replacing the variety of Rites hitherto
used, and most of the multitude of traditional service books.
Although it commanded the allegiance of a majority of the
bishops, it was almost universally unpopular. The conservative
majority, both of laity and clergy, resented the abolition of the
Mass, which had been central to much parochial piety, and
many of the Protestant minority lamented the retention of
so many traditional ceremonies. Although beautifully written
and carefully crafted, it was used only reluctantly and in
conformity to the law. The conservative Bishop of Winchester,
Stephen Gardiner, professed his willingness to use it, but
the Princess Mary rejected it scornfully, and it provoked
rebellion in Oxfordshire and the South West. The rebellions
were suppressed, and the Book of Common Prayer enforced,
but there was much evasion of its true purpose. By ignoring
the injunction to speak 'plainly and distinctly', the celebrant
could make the Communion seem very much like a traditional Mass, because the congregation would not be able to
hear what language was being used, and most of the formal
structure was the same. This cautious reform was completed
the following January by the preparation of a new Ordinal,
which was in certain respects more Protestant than the Prayer
Book. It recognised only three orders (Deacon, Priest and
Bishop), and replaced the sacramental emphasis of the priestly

[1] A priest was one who, by speaking the words of consecration, could convert
the elements of bread and wine at Communion into the physical body and
blood of Christ. Upon this mystic power his ability to absolve sins and to
intercede for sinners rested. His authority over his flock likewise depended
upon these sacramental functions. This whole Catholic perception was
rejected by Protestants, who saw the clerical function primarily in terms of
the ministry of preaching and teaching the gospel. A clergyman's authority
thus depended upon his learning and moral qualities, not upon his orders.

order with the ministry of the Gospel, by giving the ordinand a Bible in place of a paten and chalice. It retained, however, the traditional vestments for the consecration of bishops, and that led to a protracted dispute with the Reformer John Hooper, nominated to the see of Gloucester in 1551. The Prayer Book itself (or a Latin version of it) was subjected to scrutiny by two fugitive Continental Reformers, Martin Bucer and Peter Martyr, who were enjoying the hospitality of the universities at the time, and Bucer's *Censura* survives. He wrote approvingly of the Communion service and of the daily prayers, but was critical of the retention of prayers for the dead, and of liturgical gestures such as the use of the sign of the Cross in baptism. Both Bucer and Martyr urged a simplified and more unequivocally Protestant order. The intention seems to have been to submit these criticisms to Convocation in December 1550, but it is not clear that that was done. Instead a conference of bishops was assembled to consider a revised draft by Cranmer, with the young king in the background urging further reforms. Once again the result was attached as an appendix, this time to the Second Act of Uniformity, which was passed by Parliament on 14 April: 1 November being named as the day for implementation. The changes were significant. Justification was given what has been described as a 'forensic' slant, the saving grace of God being entirely external to the recipient. The order of the Communion was much simplified, the term 'Mass' altogether omitted, and the words of distribution changed to 'take and eat this in remembrance that Christ died for thee', thus shifting the whole emphasis of the service in the direction of commemoration. The burial rite was also modified to remove prayers for the dead and the invocation of the saints. The Book was already in the press when an unseemly row developed in the Council over the requirement to receive the Eucharistic elements kneeling, John Knox and John Hooper arguing that this was superstitious, and Cranmer defending his decision in terms of decency and order. Eventually it was decided to add a rubric explaining the requirement – the so-called 'Black Rubric'

– much to the archbishop's annoyance. The Second Book of Common Prayer was duly introduced in the winter of 1552–3, but the records of its reception are scanty. The Protestants may have been satisfied, but the conservative majority would have been even more discontented. However the chances are that it was imperfectly enforced because the Councillors had other things on their minds, and when, after the brief intrusion of Jane Grey, Mary secured the throne on 19 July 1553, the whole Reformed position collapsed.

For the time being 'the Queen's proceedings' merely authorized the return of the Mass in those communities which wanted it, but the first Parliament of the reign repealed the whole corpus of Edwardian legislation relating to the Church, and from 20 December 1553 the use of the Prayer Book became illegal. Missals and other service books were dug out of their hiding places, and fresh supplies imported from the continent. Leading Protestants (including the Archbishop of Canterbury) were imprisoned, and with the return of the papal jurisdiction in January 1555, a full-scale persecution commenced. Such Reformers as could escape, and could afford to do so, fled to the continent, where for the most part the exile churches either conformed to the local Protestant usage or improvised their own order. The exception was Frankfort, where a powerful Prayer Book party insisted upon the 'face of an English Church', by which they meant the 1552 Rites, which were thus preserved in use during the years under the Cross.

This party, led by Richard Cox, were among the first to return to England on the accession of Elizabeth in November 1558, and they flung themselves into the fray in defence of their Order of Service. However, Elizabeth was at first meticulous about staying within the law as it then existed, and apart from the use of the English Litany, the Mass continued unchanged in the Chapel Royal. It was not until Christmas that the Queen gave a hint of what was to come by forbidding the elevation of the Host at Mass, and by authorizing Communion in both kinds. When she was crowned in January

1559 the traditional ceremonies were used, but Elizabeth did not Communicate. On 27 December, preaching was inhibited until the order of the Church should be resolved by Parliament, and at about the same time a committee of divines sat down to revise the existing rite. There are indications that this was not easy, because the Queen and (probably) Sir William Cecil favoured the first Book of 1549, whereas most of the divines favoured the second book. The draft bills of Supremacy and Uniformity were introduced into Parliament with this issue still unresolved, although the intention of the government was clear enough from the Lord Keeper's opening speech, in which he announced that laws were to be made 'for the according and uniting of the people of the realm into an uniform order of religion ...', and in the meantime nothing should be done to encourage idolatry or superstition. It would appear that several attempts were made to introduce a revised Order of Service into Parliament during February, but each was abandoned, presumably on the grounds that it would be too controversial and what the government wanted more than anything else was a show of unity. The Bill of Uniformity ran into so much opposition in the House of Lords that Parliament was prorogued for Easter with the issue still undecided. The air was somewhat cleared by a disputation held at Westminster during the recess, which resulted in several Catholic bishops being gaoled for contempt, and apparently convinced the Queen that she would have to give way over the form of the Protestant Liturgy. When the Parliament reconvened, on 18 April, a new Bill of Uniformity was introduced, to re-establish the second Edwardian Prayer Book with certain specified amendments. It passed by the narrowest of margins, and 11 June was named as the date for the implementation of the new Order of Service.

The amendments made were verbal, and most were comparatively minor, although of considerable symbolic significance. The second rubric, which had forbidden the use of all vestments except the rochet and surplice, was replaced to permit the use of all 'such ornaments in the Church as were in use by authority of Parliament in the second year of the reign of King Edward VI', in other words 1549, before the Second Act of Uniformity. The supplication 'from the tyranny of the bishop of Rome and all his detestable enormities, Good Lord deliver us' was omitted from the Litany, and the 1549 wording was added to that of 1552 in the distribution of the Communion. This last was particularly important in that it re-introduced the possibility of a belief in the real (spiritual) presence in the elements.[2] These were all concessions in a conservative direction, reflecting the Queen's preference for 1549, and her awareness of the conservative nature of most people's religious opinions. If anyone had taken a straw poll in 1559 they would have found a substantial majority in favour of 'religion as king Henry left it', but that was no longer an option, and Elizabeth was clearly concerned to mitigate the harshness of the 1552 Rite. She did this in various other ways, to the disgust of her more zealous bishops, encouraging church music through the Chapel Royal, and the use of candles and a cross upon the Communion table. Altars were outlawed, as they had been in the latter part of Edward VI's reign, but discretion was exercised over the positioning of the Communion table, which was often located 'altar wise' at the east end of the church. Meanwhile the English Bible, which was an essential partner to the vernacular liturgy, had been through a number of revisions. First the Great Bible had been authorized in 1539, then the Geneva Bible, not authorized but widely used, which followed the Marian exile in 1560, and finally the Bishops' Bible of 1568, which was introduced as a deliberate counter to the Geneva version, many of the marginalia of which were deemed unacceptable by the orthodox. Although the 1559 settlement appears to have been accepted quietly enough, and only some 300 incumbents were deprived over the next five years for their

---

[2] The 1552 Rite had implied a simple commemoration, although it seems that Cranmer was not committed to that interpretation. The words 'The body of Christ, given for you ...' restored the balance.

refusal to conform, by 1570 there was considerable tension within the English Church. To this tension the Prayer Book was central, being described by one Puritan as 'culled out of that popish dunghill the Mass, full of abominations'. This was an extreme view, but many were dissatisfied with it, and the ornaments rubric, for example, was virtually abandoned. The Queen, however, defended it with great tenacity, at least twice ordering Parliament to cease discussing alternatives, and her position became somewhat easier when the more vociferous Puritans embraced a Presbyterian position which clearly attacked the Royal Supremacy. By the 1590s, the Prayer Book had developed a momentum of its own, having become in the eyes of conformists not only a symbol of loyalty to the 'English way' in religion, but also of loyalty to Elizabeth. There may well have been Puritans who hankered after the Scottish or Genevan practices, just as there were Church papists who would have preferred the Roman Rite, but it was not difficult to represent all such Dissenters as being 'un-English'. Whereas in 1549 or 1552 the Protestant orders seemed, to many, to be German or Swiss imports in spite of the use of English, by the 1590s the 1559 Rite had been absorbed into the English national consciousness, and become synonymous with loyalty to the crown.

Because of his Calvinist background, and the use of the Genevan-based Book of Common Order in Scotland, the accession of James I revived Puritan hopes of securing some amendment to the Common Prayer, and the so-called Millenary Petition was presented to him for that purpose within a month of his coming to the throne. James, who was savouring his new authority as Supreme Head of the Church, convened the Westminster Conference in January 1604, against the advice of his senior clergy, to consider this petition, and much enjoyed arbitrating the resultant disagreements. In terms of the Prayer Book the results were minimal, but not without significance. The rubrics for baptism were altered to restrict the rite to authorized ministers, and explanations were offered in the service of confirmation. Some additions were made to the Catechism, and the prayers of intercession for the Royal family were added to take account of the fact that the king now had a wife and children. The rearrangements did not really touch the core concerns of the petitioners, which were mainly to do with the use of liturgical gestures, such as the sign of the Cross, but they were as much as could be obtained. The main outcome of the conference was a resolution to proceed with a new authorized translation of the Bible, which was put in hand shortly after. The result was published in 1611 as the King James Version, which thereafter replaced both the Genevan Bible and the Bishops Bible, the publication of which was discontinued. James liked the Church of England, and sought to extend its practices to his homeland. In 1610 he restored the episcopate to the Kirk and in 1616 obtained the consent of the General Assembly to the issuing of a Prayer Book. However, grass-roots resistance proved to be too strong and the resulting Form of Service remained in manuscript. It was not until 1633 that his son Charles, visiting Edinburgh for his Scottish coronation, brought the English Prayer Book with him, and the storm that resulted destabilized his government north of the border. In England the modified 1604 version continued in use until the Civil War.

English, or its Scottish variant, was of course the main vernacular spoken in the British Isles, but it was not the only one. A translation of the 1549 Prayer Book into (somewhat idiosyncratic) Welsh appeared in the same year, and a more usable version accompanied the Welsh New Testament in 1567. It was recognized that English was not spoken through most of Wales, and that the successful evangelisation of the country depended upon vernacular sermons and a vernacular liturgy. This need took precedence over English cultural imperialism and the worship of the Church in Wales went straight from Latin to Welsh, without passing through English on the way. In the Channel Islands, the 1552 Liturgy was translated into French by order of Sir Hugh Paulet, the Governor of Calais, and French translations continued to track the English versions down to the seventeenth century. There was even a Latin version of 1559, explicitly approved for use in the universities, where the vernacular was not approved, even for conversations! The biggest omission in this respect was in Ireland, where the Protestant Rite continued throughout the sixteenth century to be a symbol of the English political ascendancy. The Gaelic-speaking Irish, who formed the vast majority of the population, continued in the Latin Rite and the Roman obedience, and attempts at integration were handicapped by the absence of an acceptable Irish version of the Prayer Book. This lack was not remedied until 1608, while a Gaelic translation of the New Testament, which had been put in hand in 1567, did not finally appear until 1603. By that time it was far too late to spread the Reformation to the greater part of Ireland, and religious division continued to bedevil that country until the Civil War – and for long after. The English Prayer Book was, and remained, a symbol of Protestantism: and that, in Ireland, meant a colonial ascendancy.

Meanwhile, in England, it had become the hallmark of Anglican conformity, which was why an Ordinance of Parliament terminated its use on 3 January 1645. It had become too closely associated with the government of the Church by bishops, and that, for the time being, was unacceptable to the dominant party.

Section 2

The Language of the Book of Common Prayer

Through all the Changing Scenes of Life: Living with the Prayer Book

P. D. James

P. D. James was born in Oxford in 1920 and educated at Cambridge High School. She is the author of eighteen crime novels and three non-fiction books, and is President of the Society of Authors. She worked in the National Health Service and the Home Office, retiring in 1979. She is a Fellow of the Royal Society of Literature and of the Royal Society of Arts, and has seven honorary doctorates from British universities. She was awarded an OBE in 1983 and created a life peer in 1991. From childhood she has been a lover of the Book of Common Prayer and is an enthusiast for its continued use. She has two daughters, five grandchildren and seven great-grandchildren.

Those of us who first encountered and loved the Book of Common Prayer in early childhood are indeed fortunate and my experience of this marvellous book began long before I could understand the words. When they first married, my parents lived in Oxford, where in 1920 I was born, and as both had a deep affection for church music, they would frequently attend Sung Evensong in the college chapels as well as services in the cathedral, and I would be carried there in my mother's arms. Thus listening to church music and hearing the liturgy were two of my very early and formative experiences. And later, when we moved from Oxford to Ludlow on the

Welsh borders, I would be taken with my brother and sister every Sunday to Evensong, one of the most satisfying services of the church spiritually and aesthetically, and still, I think, my favourite. We attended a small church near Ludford Bridge by the Teme where in winter there was a coke-burning stove which would flare when the wind changed, reminding me of the tongues of flame at Whitsun. In those days we would carry our Prayer Books to church and when I could read I occupied myself during the *longueurs* of the sermons, which I was too young to understand, in exploring the beauty, the history and the romance of the Prayer Book. It is, of course, the book of an agricultural and island race, with its prayers for fine weather and 'such moderate rain and showers, that we may receive the fruits of the earth to our comfort'; its gratitude that after a plague of immoderate rain God 'has relieved and comforted our souls by this seasonal blessed change of weather'; and its petitions for deliverance at sea from storm, tempest and the enemy. I can remember first reading the words at the end of the Communion of the Sick: 'In the time of the plague, sweat, or such other like contagious times of sickness or diseases, when none of the Parish or neighbours can be gotten to communicate with the sick in their houses, for fear of the infection, upon special request of the diseased, the Minister may only communicate with him', and thinking of the priestly heroism which that act envisaged, the parish clergyman carrying the sacred vessels through the deserted street of the stricken village to share a communion which he knew would almost certainly be his last. Later I went to a church school in Ludlow where the parish priest would visit each week to teach us the Collect for the week and instruct us in its meaning. So those marvellous prayers, at once so beautifully constructed, so simple and yet so full of meaning, entered early into my consciousness to become part of my religious and literary heritage and, with the King James Bible, helped to make me a writer.

Later we moved to Cambridge and it was King's College Chapel which, during the years of early adolescence, provided for me my most meaningful religious experience. I recall the solemnity, the grandeur and the beauty of the building, the high soaring magnificence of the roof, the candlelit gloom, the decorous procession of the boys of the choir, the order and the beauty of the traditional service. I probably realized even then that I was in danger of confusing the worship of God with a strong emotional and aesthetic response to architecture, music and literature, but it seemed to me that God should be worshipped in the beauty of holiness.

In the beginning was the Word. And the words of our public liturgy, in their beauty, their truth, their numinous power, should be capable of so entering our consciousness that we do not need to search for them, but can release the mind to enter into stillness which is the heart of prayer and worship. By the accident of history – or perhaps it would be more accurate to say by the grace of God – the English Prayer Book was produced by a man who was a genius in the writing of English prose. Cranmer, and the Commission of which he was a part, set up originally in the reign of Edward VI, produced successive books in 1549 and 1552, but it is the final text of 1662 which became the Book of Common Prayer and Cranmer's most lasting memorial.

Cranmer's life was one of politics and court intrigue as well as religion, more varied and dangerously influential in the palaces of power than that of the scholar Tyndale. He rose rapidly in the favour of Henry VIII, to whom he was always loyal and whom he supported both in the King's protracted efforts to achieve divorce from his first wife and in his assumption of the role of Head of the Church. Not surprisingly, his Reformist sympathies made him a much-hated adversary of Queen Mary, which led to his martyrdom on 21 March 1556. For many people he is probably chiefly remembered for that last account of his life when he held his right hand in the flames because it had written his recantation and deserved first to feel the fire. It was the same hand, moving patiently over the pages that had given England the incomparable Book of Common Prayer. Cranmer was principally a borrower and an arranger, humble enough to recognize and use what he could not hope to improve. He took from Miles Coverdale, George Joye and Richard Taverner, always with an unerring ear for what was memorable and eternal. He had an impeccable ear, balancing the sturdiness of the vernacular with the more complicated Italianate words so that every clause has its subtle and graceful rhythm. He is one of the greatest influences on our language, our religion and our culture.

The *Oxford Dictionary of Quotations* has an index of 70,000, and there are 13 sources whose words are most quoted, including the Bible and the Prayer Book. There are 396 entries from the Prayer Book and we have only to read these pages to realize how many expressions of our common speech derive from the Prayer Book and how often in our reading of poetry or novels we can see how many talented writers have the words of the Prayer Book imprinted on their minds. We can recognize the Prayer Book's cadences in the works of Isaac Walton and John Bunyan, in the majestic phrases of John Milton, Sir Thomas Browne and Edward Gibbon. We can see its echo in the works of such very different writers as Daniel Defoe, Thackeray, the Brontës, Coleridge, T. S. Eliot and even Dorothy L. Sayers. It is difficult to see how anyone can seriously study our history or our literature without reference to the Book of Common Prayer.

In the words of Cranmer's biographer Diarmaid MacCulloch, 'Millions who have never heard of Cranmer, or of the muddled heroism of his death, have echoes of his words in their minds'. And this is what the words of the Prayer Book supremely do: they echo in the mind. And not only in the individual mind, but in the corporate mind of the Church, indeed in the mind of the nation. Thus echoing and thus safely lodged they provide a source of spiritual nourishment and comfort throughout all the vicissitudes of life, particularly at times of danger and distress and in the hour of death. 'Suffer us not, at our last hour, for any pains of death, to fall from thee'. The words come so easily to mind. 'We have erred and strayed from Thy ways like lost sheep. We have followed too much the devices and desires of our own hearts'. 'We bless thee for our creation, preservation, and all the blessings of this life; but above all for thine inestimable love in the redemption of the world by our Lord Jesus Christ, for the means of grace, and for the hope of glory'. And the evening prayer, 'Lighten our darkness, we beseech thee, O Lord; and by thy great mercy defend us from all perils and dangers of this night'. Surely this is as relevant to an elderly woman alone in her inner-city bed, indeed to us all, as it was to the people who first heard it in an age as troubled as our own. And the invitation to Holy Communion: 'Ye that do truly and earnestly repent you of your sins, and are in love and charity with your neighbours, and intend to lead a new life, following the commandments of God, and walking from henceforth in his holy ways: Draw near with faith, and take this holy Sacrament to your comfort; and make your humble confession to Almighty God, meekly kneeling upon your knees'.

This is surely intelligible, needing no alteration to make it meaningful to a twenty-first century congregation. It is meant to be spoken aloud by a priest. It is memorable in its balanced cadences so that, hearing it again and again, as our ancestors heard it over the centuries, the words enter into our consciousness and become a living part of our religious life and heritage. Of course the language of our liturgy will continue to change. I'm not suggesting that no one should ever write a new prayer. But we should change it, not by throwing out what has superbly stood the test of centuries, but by adding with discretion and with humility, offering to God in worship always the best of which we are capable. The candle of Cranmer's Book of Common Prayer has burned with a steady light for over 300 years. Finally to cast it away or lose it by deliberate neglect would be an act of liturgical vandalism for which our century would not be forgiven.

Common Worship, which has replaced the unlamented Alternative Service Book, does at least contain portions of Cranmer's Prayer Book, but they are not easy to find. Common

Worship, in its huge variety, is more a source book, a liturgical pick and mix from which parish priests can select parts which take their fancy and put them together in a pamphlet. No one can possibly carry Common Worship to church as once we carried our Prayer Book, nor indeed find their way through it if they did. I am reminded of those words in the Preface to the 1662 Prayer Book setting out the justification for a new liturgy and drawing attention to the repetitions and confusion of the existing books for public worship. 'Moreover, the number and hardness of the Rules ..., and the manifold changings of the Service, was the cause, that to turn the Book only was so hard and intricate a matter, that many times there was more business to find out what should be read, than to read it when it was found out'. Seventeenth-century words as true, alas, today as when they were written.

In considering liturgy and language, we have now a new complication which was unlikely to worry revisers in previous centuries – the influence of the feminists in the Church of England and in society generally, who feel strongly that inclusive language should be introduced into the Prayer Book. But surely we never think of God in terms of gender. We know that God is not male any more than God is female. The first Article of the Articles of Religion in the Prayer Book boldly attempts a definition, words used to express the inexpressible. 'There is but one living and true God, everlasting, without body, parts, or passions; of infinite power, wisdom, and goodness; the Maker, and Preserver of all things both visible and invisible'. God is spirit and they who worship Him must worship Him in spirit and in truth. I am no theologian, but I do not think there has ever been a heresy which proclaimed that God became incarnate to redeem only males. It follows that the words 'man' and 'mankind' in Scripture and in the Prayer Book must always have meant the whole of humanity. If we give way to the demand that 'man' and 'mankind' must always be changed to 'man and woman' or 'humankind', we shall gradually come to lose the comprehensive meaning of 'man' and 'mankind' and be forced into a wholesale revision of our liturgy and scripture which would be in danger of perverting both language and theology.

We live in an age notable for a kind of fashionable silliness and imbued with a restless desire for change. It sometimes seems that nothing old, nothing well-established, nothing which has evolved through centuries of experience and loving use escapes our urge to diminish, revise or abolish it. Above all every organisation has to be relevant – a very fashionable word – to the needs of modern life, as if human beings in the twenty-first century are somehow fundamentally different in their needs and aspirations from all previous generations. A country which ceases to value and learn from its history, neglects its language and literature, despises its traditions and is unified only by a common frenetic drive for getting and spending and for material wealth, will lose more than its nationhood; it will lose its soul. Let us cherish and use what we still precariously hold. Let us strive to ensure that what has been handed down to us is not lost to generations to come.

I should like to end with one of my favourite prayers, the Fifth Collect after the Communion Service:

Almighty God, the fountain of all wisdom, who knowest our necessities before we ask, and our ignorance in asking: We beseech thee to have compassion upon our infirmities; and those things, which for our unworthiness we dare not, and for our blindness we cannot ask, vouchsafe to give us for the worthiness of thy Son Jesus Christ our Lord. *Amen.*

Something Understood

David Curry

A graduate of the University of King's College, Halifax, Dalhousie University, Harvard University, and Trinity College, University of Toronto, the **Revd David Curry** was ordained to the priesthood in 1982. He is currently the Rector of the Anglican Parish of Christ Church, Windsor, Nova Scotia and Chaplain and Senior School English and Philosophy teacher in the International Baccalaureate programme at King's-Edgehill School. Vice-Chairman of the Prayer Book Society of Canada, he has spoken and written on matters of theology, liturgy, history and literature. He and his wife Marilyn live in Falmouth, Nova Scotia. They have three children; Elizabeth, Joel and Madeleine.

Introduction

'It was not for me to bandy civilities with my Sovereign',[1] Dr Samuel Johnson famously said, having been asked about his audience in 1767 with King George III. His remark captures a sensibility about language that is very much in keeping with the Book of Common Prayer. It emphatically does not bandy civilities with God.

Refined, austere, magisterial and elevated in its tone of address, the language of the Book of Common Prayer is language that takes seriously the awesome majesty of God and the wonder of the human desire to pray and serve the God

---

[1] James Boswell, *Life of Johnson*, ed. George Birbeck Hill (1934), Oxford: Clarendon Press, vol. 2, p. 21.

'whose service is perfect freedom'. The language of the Prayer Book is dignified and intense, intimate and precise at the same time. It is the language of prayer and theology.

Poetry and prayer; theology as prayer; prayer as 'something understood',[2] to use George's Herbert's phrase about prayer itself; and language that is memorable: all these are features of the language of the Book of Common Prayer that warrant its regard and occasion its celebration.

The language of the Book of Common Prayer is prose that borders on poetry, prose that is almost on the verge of bursting into song. Its powerful language shapes and instils an understanding of the truth and the beauty of God in the soul. Like the King James Bible, the Prayer Book, too, is almost deliberately archaic in its voice and expression. It is emphatically not the street talk of any age of the English language.

There is, perhaps, no idea more mistaken than the assumption that the Liturgy translated into the vernacular tongues of the newly emergent European nation states meant a commitment to the banal and the everyday, to the idiomatic or the conventional. No: in a language 'understanded of the people' (Article XXIV) meant in a language that everyone was capable of being taught; not something immediately acquired. And unlike the King James Bible and Shakespeare's poems and plays, the archaic terms and expressions of the Book of Common Prayer are really quite minimal. In short, it is capable of being understood.

But which Book of Common Prayer? The mother book of the Books of Common Prayer that has shaped the spirituality and outlook of so many in the British Empire and Commonwealth is the 1662 Book of Common Prayer. It looked back to its antecedents, to the architect of the Common Prayer tradition, Archbishop Thomas Cranmer, and the Books of 1549 and 1552 under his authorship; it looked back to the 1559 Book of Common Prayer that belonged to

---

[2] George Herbert, 'Prayer (I)' in *The Temple*, Oxford: Oxford University Press (1961), p. 44.

the Elizabethan Settlement in religion and which received its finest *apologia* at the hand of one of England's greatest theologians, the judicious Richard Hooker. It looked back to the 1604 Book of Common Prayer that belonged to the early days of the reign of King James. And it was, if nothing else, a conservative revision undertaken in the wake of the disruptions and confusions of the English Civil War when bishops and prayer books were both proscribed.

Cranmer's Book(s) of Common Prayer, the Works of Shakespeare and the King James Bible are the three great monuments of early modern English that have influenced the character and development of the English language. David Crystal has argued that the influence on the development of the English language by the King James Bible far exceeds that of the Works of Shakespeare.[3] He says very little about the influence of the Book of Common Prayer. And yet, the influence of the King James Bible is almost inseparable from the Prayer Book. The 1662 Book of Common Prayer, for instance, made the change from the Great Bible translation to the King James Bible for the Epistles and Gospels contained therein, making the Book of Common Prayer one of the major conduits for the communication of New Testament passages of the King James Bible to a larger world.

But not the Psalter. Somehow, Miles Coverdale's version of the Psalter (1535) used in the Great Bible remained and was not replaced by the King James Bible version of the Psalms. An oversight? No. The recognition, perhaps, of the inherent memorableness of its structure and phrasing? We may never know. All that the note in the Preface says, is 'that the Psalter followeth the Division of the Hebrews, and the Translation of the great English Bible, set forth and used in the time of King Henry the Eighth and Edward the Sixth'.

---

[3] David Crystal (2010), *Begat: The King James Bible & the English Language*, Oxford: Oxford University Press, p. 258.

But it raises intriguing questions about language, its strength and power, something about which Cranmer himself was only too acutely aware. Words and phrases mean everything.

The Language of Prayer

'Prayer signifies even all the service that we ever do unto God',[4] Richard Hooker observes. The language of the Prayer Book expresses fully that Godward intent of our lives. Prayer is the Godward direction of our heart's desires and it places us with God. Rendering that primary intent into vigorous and concise English, free of unnecessary ornament and affectation, was Cranmer's constant aim and struggle.

The architect of the Book of Common Prayer, Cranmer drew upon many, many sources, both ancient and modern. It was not a one-man production, nor could it be. Yet his was the dominant hand in terms of editorship and translation into English of a variety of liturgical sources that has resulted in the Book of Common Prayer and, especially, in terms of its Reformed emphasis.

To him we owe the resonances and cadences of the Litany and the eloquence and concision of the Collects as well as many a felicitous turn of phrase in the Liturgy of the Book of Common Prayer that is at once arresting and memorable.

The Litany

The Litany, composed in 1544 and authorized for use in 1545, provides a marvellous instruction about prayer that is scriptural and creedal and that draws upon a host of traditional sources as well. It begins with an address to God, first, in terms of the distinctions of the divine persons, Father, Son, and Holy Ghost, and, then, in the unity of the divine nature. An instinct for rhythm and balance meant adding a creedal element to the invocation of the Holy Ghost which the Latin Litany did not provide. 'O God the

---

[4] Richard Hooker, *Lawes of Ecclesiastical Polity, Book V*, 7th ed., arr. J. Keble, revised by Church and Paget, New York: Burt Franklin, Vol. II, p. 115.

Father of heaven … O God the Son, Redeemer of the world'
is balanced with 'O God the Holy Ghost, proceeding from
the Father and the Son', a direct creedal reference to the
western form of the Nicene Creed. This is further underlined
by a similar elaboration in the invocation of the Trinity itself
which explicitly echoes the language and understanding of
the Athanasian Creed: 'O holy, blessed, and glorious Trinity,
three Persons and one God'.

Prayer is addressed directly and clearly to the God who
has revealed himself as the Father, the Son and the Holy
Ghost. One of the features of the Book of Common Prayer
is the language of clarity about the God whom we address.
This early exercise in translation and adaptation shows a
characteristic impulse that runs through all the prayers of the
Prayer Book, namely, an adherence to Trinitarian orthodoxy
in its Western understanding and to the divine attributes of
God of classical theology. Prayer is not made to 'whomever it
may concern' or to 'the God of x and y', filling in the blanks
with adjectives of our own devising. God is addressed in the
confidence of the Scriptural and Creedal understanding of
Revelation.

This clarity and directness of address to God in his Triune
majesty in the Litany is complemented by a compact series of
prayers. These are marvels of concision and comprehension.
They compass the whole range of the human condition with
respect to the forms and varieties of sinfulness as well as all
the sorts and conditions of human need.

It has been the work of generations of scholars to track
down and analyse the various sources which Cranmer may
have used. What that scholarship equally reveals is the
judicious and creative adaptation of a great variety of sources
to compose a compelling pattern of prayer that is intense,
instructive and deeply devotional. It is also creedally focused.
In the prayers for deliverance we go from the enumeration
of all the forms of suffering and misery to the recitation of
the creedal articles of the means of our salvation; the shift
is signalled in the change of prepositions; 'from' to 'by'. The

saving work of Christ is central. The language is strong and
vigorous and has a rhythm, power, and force in the gathering
up of complementary phrases.

For example, the Litany bids us pray that we may be
delivered 'from all blindness of heart; from pride, vain-glory,
and hypocrisy; from envy, hatred and malice, and all unchari-
tableness', a pretty concise and yet restrained summary of
the disorders of the human heart that echoes the moral and
theological tradition of the classification of the seven deadly
sins, further elaborated in the next petition that prays for
deliverance 'from fornication, and all other deadly sins',
only to recall the explicit renunciations that belong to the
baptismal service, namely, 'the deceits of the world, the flesh
and the devil'.

Only then does the Litany go on to name the forms of
suffering that arise from the disorders of nature: 'from lightening and tempest, from plague, pestilence, and famine',
all matters that belong to our world and day. But, then, in
mid-petition, we are reminded of the connection between
those forms of suffering and the forms of suffering that arise
from the disorders of the human heart; we pray for deliverance 'from battle and murder, and from sudden death'. In
the next petition, the forms of civil and ecclesiastical disorder
are invoked, 'all sedition, privy conspiracy, and rebellion', on
the one hand, and, 'all false doctrine, heresy, and schism', on
the other hand, concluding with the concise explication of the
underlying spiritual malady, namely, our 'hardness of heart'
and our 'contempt of thy Word and Commandment'. Once
again, precise, clear and direct.

How shall we be delivered from such a parade of natural,
political, social and psychological evils? Only by the grace of
Christ which the Litany then rehearses in a creedal way: 'by
the mystery of thy holy Incarnation; by thy holy Nativity and
Circumcision; by thy Baptism, Fasting, and Temptation', a
double sequence of doctrinal triplets that is then complemented
by a quartet of doctrinal couplets: 'by thine Agony and bloody
Sweat; by thy Cross and Passion; by thy precious Death and

Burial; by thy glorious Resurrection and Ascension', ending on
the single doctrinal note, 'by the coming of the Holy Ghost'.

The Litany proceeds to offer an ordered sequence of inter-
cessions: for the governance of the Church universal; for the
King; for the Royal Family; for the illumination of all Bishops,
Priests and Deacons; for the Lords of the Council and all
Nobility; and for Magistrates; in short, for those in authority.
It, then, intercedes for all people in terms of their spiritual
and temporal needs, with specific reference to the 'fatherless
children, and widows, and all that are desolate and oppressed'.

This sense and sensibility about balance and rhythm, about
rhetoric in the service of piety and devotion under the guidance
of creedal doctrine, illustrates something of the power of the
Prayer Book language of prayer. Many of the alterations
and variations that have occurred in the daughter books of
Common Prayer pay homage to their maternal origins even in
their adaptations. Its rhythms and patterns are ever there to be
reclaimed and remembered.

The whole Litany ends with the Prayer of St Chrysostom
which would later be incorporated into other parts of the
Liturgy, particularly the offices of Morning and Evening
Prayer. Cranmer translated this, not from the original Greek,
but from a 1528 Latin version that originated in Venice. It,
too, has become one of the beloved prayers of the Prayer
Book tradition by virtue of its theological language about the
nature of prayer itself. Once again, there is that strong sense
of the objectivity of God and his will for us that conditions
and enables our prayers to be truly prayers 'as may be most
expedient for [us]'; in short, prayer that seeks the will of God
for us not out of sense of entitlement and demand but out of
a confidence in the loving mercy of God that he will grant
us 'in this world knowledge of thy truth, and in the world to
come life everlasting'. The Litany ends with 'the Grace' derived
from 2 Cor. 13.14, another testimony to the centrality of the
Scriptures in the shaping of prayer and worship.

The Collects

George Herbert's poem, *Ungratefulnesse*, illustrates something of the dynamic interplay between doctrine and devotion that is the living breath of the Book of Common Prayer best captured, perhaps, in the language of its Collects.

> Thou hast but two rare cabinets full of treasure,
>   The Trinitie, and Incarnation:
>   Thou hast unlockt them both,
>   And made them jewels to betroth
>   The work of thy creation
> Unto thy self in everlasting pleasure.[5]

The Collects are masterpieces of doctrinal concision. Like the Litany, they are clear and precise in their address and, like the Litany, they place the needs of our humanity in an ordered relation to God's will precisely out of this sensibility about doctrine and devotion. As in Herbert's verse, the Collects reveal the doctrine of the Trinity and the Incarnation as the true basis of our prayer that seeks the perfection of the divine creation and God's enjoyment of our humanity in him. The Collects are, as Diarmaid McCulloch observes, the 'jewelled miniatures [that] are one of the chief glories of the Anglican liturgical tradition, a particularly distinguished development of the genre of brief prayer which is peculiar to the Western Church'.[6] Nowhere, perhaps, does the linguistical genius of Cranmer stand out more clearly than in the Collects. They are prayable, thinkable, comprehensible and sound.

The Collects reveal much about the language of prayer in the Book of Common Prayer as developed by Cranmer. McCulloch offers a magisterial comment about the Collects. 'They exhibit the characteristic three-fold nature of Cranmer's liturgical compilations: adaptation of ancient examples in his

---

[5] Herbert, 'Ungratefulnesse' in *The Temple*, p. 73.
[6] Diarmaid McCulloch (1996), *Thomas Cranmer: A Life*, Yale University Press, New Haven & London, p. 417.

own English translation (sixty-seven collects with origins in the Sarum rite alone), refinement of existing translations and new texts from contemporaries, and straightforward original compositions, [namely] twenty-four purely original collects'.[7] Among their distinguishing features is the deliberate and intentional incorporation of the language of Scripture into the language of prayer. Not only is the Prayer Book 80 per cent Scripture; it is a way of praying the Scriptures.

That sensibility is best illustrated in one of the best known of the Cranmerian Collects, the Collect for the Second Sunday in Advent. It expresses and embodies a kind of theology of Revelation and is drawn explicitly from the Epistle and Gospel for the day.

> Blessed Lord, who hast caused all holy Scriptures to bee written for our learnyng; graunte us that we maye in suche wise heare them, read, marke, learne and inwardly digeste them, that by pacience and coumfort of thy holy woorde, we may embrace, and ever holde fast the blessed hope of euerlasting life, which thou hast geuen us in our sauiour Jesus Christe.[8]

Apart from the changes in the spelling towards a more standardized form, the only other change effected in 1662 was the omission of the pronoun 'us' in the second clause.

In other cases, Cranmer often shows a fine touch for the little alteration that makes all the difference, as McCulloch notes about the Collect for Peace at Evensong. Cranmer kept Robert Redman's opening line: 'O God, from whom all holy desires, all good counsels, and all just works do proceed', but altered the rest to achieve an even more finely balanced and effectively expressed rendition. 'Give unto us thy servants that peace which the world cannot give, that both our hearts may

---

[7] McCulloch, op. cit., p. 417.
[8] *The First and Second Prayer Book of King Edward IV*, London: J. M Dent & Sons (1968), Everyman's Library Edition, reprinted 1975, p. 34.

be set to obey thy commandments, and also that by thee, we being defended from the fear of our enemies, may pass our time in rest and quietness, through the merits of Jesu[sic] Christ our saviour'. The changes are few but effective, a deft literary touch, not unlike the touches that belong to the King James Bible.

Not all of the Collects in the 1662 Book of Common Prayer are Cranmer's. There is a post-Cranmerian development that is also an important feature of the 1662 Book. John Cosin, Bishop of Durham, contributed the Collect for the Third Sunday in Advent and the Sixth Sunday after Epiphany, following what he took to be Cranmer's example, namely, prayers that draw upon the language of the Scripture readings, effectively providing a way of praying the Scriptures in their creedal or doctrinal sense.

The Collects embody a theological sensibility. Scripture is a doctrinal instrument of salvation. The Collects of Cranmer and Cosin bear eloquent testimony to this feature of the Book of Common Prayer. There is a unity of literature and theology.

The Language of Theology

Style has become a feature of the liturgical debates in more contemporary times. The distinction or separation between the aesthetical and the theological is part of the history of the reception of the Book of Common Prayer. To separate style from substance would be almost unthinkable for Cranmer and for those engaged in the re-establishment of the Prayer Book in 1662. There is the paradox that the Book of Common Prayer has often been celebrated for the beauty of its prose and expression by those who have the least commitment to its teaching, such as the literary atheist, Philip Pullman.[9] The same paradox, of course, is there for the various aficionados of the King James Bible.

Doris Lessing, in being asked to write an introduction to Ecclesiastes in the ingenious Pocket Canons series, had to

---

[9] As in the 17 March 2009, *Sunday Times* article by Alan Franks.

admit that she had never read it before but recalled the observation of her father about having to go to Church three times
on Sunday plus Sunday School. It seemed 'like a great black
hole every week', he told her, and yet 'it was listening to the
prose of the Bible and the prayer book that taught him to love
language and good literature'.[10] Somehow that observation
stayed with her with respect to the language of the King James
Bible and the language of the Book of Common Prayer.

Language matters but not just in terms of style and
expression. It matters because of what it has to say, not just
how it says it. Cranmer himself was only too well aware of
the power of language to shape a religious culture and nation.
The theological and the political were intimately entwined in
ways that we find almost impossible to conceive. Cranmer's
translation of the Latin Collects was in part an exercise about
determining a theological and doctrinal outlook. There was a
theological programme that is an inescapable feature of the
language of prayer. It was not merely a matter of style and
effect.

No phrase better captures the theology of the English
Church expressed in her Liturgy than the Preface to the
1662 Book of Common Prayer. 'It has been the wisdom of
the Church of England ever since the first compiling of her
Publick Liturgy, to keep the mean between the two extremes,
of too much stiffness in refusing, and of too much easiness
in admitting any variation from it'. It states the fundamentally conservative feature of every Prayer Book revision that
remains within the orbit of the classical Books of Common
Prayer.

The Savoy Conference was convened in 1661 to consider a
variety of suggestions about the Liturgy of the English Church
after the English Civil War or Interregnum, suggestions arising
from both the Presbyterian or Puritan elements formerly in
the ascendency during that period and from what some have

[10] Doris Lessing (1998), *Introduction to Ecclesiastes*, Pocket Canons Series,
New York: Grove Press, p. ix.

called the Laudian elements in the English Church. Of the 96
suggestions made by Richard Baxter *et al.* of the Puritan wing,
only eighteen were adopted, but it was equally the case that
very few of the liturgical changes promoted in the Durham
Book of John Cosin were adopted either.

The intent was about 'keep[ing] the mean', a doctrinal
mean, and one which reflected the essentially Reformed basis
of the Book of Common Prayer. The Latin Collects bore
already the distinct influence of Augustine's emphasis on
God's grace against the Pelagian and semi-Pelagian views that
located a self-sufficient moral principle within us.

This complemented Cranmer's Reformed view about faith
and works. The major theological changes to the Latin
Collects concerned removing from consideration any sense
of our meriting God's grace. Its use would be constrained
deliberately to the person of Jesus Christ as in the Collect for
First Sunday after Easter and the Collects for the Twelfth and
Thirteenth Sundays after Trinity. Original compositions, like
the Collect for the Feast of St Luke composed in 1549 and
the Collect for Easter Even incorporated in the 1662 Book of
Common Prayer, reveal the same theological emphasis.

Gerlach Flicke's 1545 iconic painting of Thomas Cranmer
captures the theological intent expressed in the language of
the Book(s) of Common Prayer. Cranmer is pictured reading
a volume of the Epistles of St Paul while before him on a
table are two books, one title of which can be clearly seen.
It is Augustine's treatise *De Fides et Operibus*, 'On Faith and
Works'. As McCulloch suggests, this expresses the nature of
the theological programme that underlies the enterprise of the
Book(s) of Common Prayer. It would be about the primacy
of the Scriptures understood through the best of Patristic
scholarship, particularly Augustine; in short, a 'Protestant
Augustinianism'[11] was a distinct feature of the Reformed

[11] Ashley Null (1994), from an unpublished Cambridge Ph.D dissertation,
Thomas Cranmer's Doctrine of Repentance, quoted in McCulloch, op. cit.,
p. 374.

Theology of the Book of Common Prayer. As Stephen Hampton has argued 'the Reformed theological tradition is an essential ingredient in any conception of Anglicanism'.[12]

The 1662 Book of Common Prayer maintained an essentially Reformed perspective. Latter-day Latitudinarians, influenced by Armininianism and Socinianism, would attempt to undermine the Reformed theology of grace and the centrality of the Trinity, attempting to remove the Athanasian Trinitarian references from the Prayer Book.[13] The 1662 BCP has stood as a kind of bulwark of essential orthodoxy against such agendas. Hampton observes that the Anglican Reformed tradition 'continued to insist upon the evangelical teaching of justification by faith alone, upon the established scholastic way of expressing Trinitarian doctrine, and upon the broadly Thomist understanding of the divine nature which was shared by both Roman Catholic and Reformed theologians'.[14] Those points of theological emphasis are a critical feature of the 1662 Book of Common Prayer expressed in the language of prayer.

The poet, writer and lay theologian Charles Williams, in his play *Thomas Cranmer of Canterbury* captures succinctly and wonderfully the distinctiveness of the man and the book. More than simply 'the bless'd beauty of the shaped syllables'[15] by which 'the Word takes the sound natively around',[16] what we might call the aesthetic approach, Cranmer's poetic language 'enfranchise(s) Christ into English speech'. Williams has grasped the theological intention of the endeavour itself.

---

[12] Stephen Hampton (2008), *Anti-Arminians: The Anglican Reformed Tradition from Charles II to George I*, Oxford Theological Monographs, Oxford: Oxford University Press, p. 273.

[13] See Philip Dixon (2003), *Nice and Hot Disputes: The Doctrine of the Trinity in the Seventeenth Century*, London and New York: T & T Clark.

[14] Hampton, op. cit., p. 272.

[15] Charles Williams (1963), *Thomas Cranmer of Canterbury in Collected Plays*, London: Oxford University Press, p. 4.

[16] Williams, op.cit., p. 20.

O but this – that words be as muscles and veins
to Christ's Spirit bringing communion, the shape
of his advent, nor none there to escape
into the unformed shadow of mystery mere,
but find a strong order, a diagram clear,
a ladder runged and tongued; now my hand,
my unworthy hand, shall set itself to that end.
Be for the need of the land the ritual penned.[17]

As Williams has one character put it, 'There is this to be said
for my lord of Canterbury,/he dimly believes in something
outside himself ... which is more, I can tell you,' he says to the
audience, 'than most of you do'.[18]

The Language of Instruction

The language of worship is equally the language of instruction.
In the Liturgy, we engage God with the whole of our being
and that includes our minds. There is a didactic character to
certain features of the Book of Common Prayer expressed
in the Catechism, in the various Exhortations, and in the
structure of the services themselves. Why?

Because the language of the Prayer Book is about the
dynamic between justification and sanctification understood
through the distinctive lenses of the English Reformation. In its
doctrinal minimalism there is a distinctive emphasis upon the
nature of our incorporation into Christ expressed in terms of
the interplay between justification and sanctification. The task
of holding together these two sides of our life in Christ belongs
to the continuing dialectic of the Church's life of prayer. On
the one hand, there is the constant thrust upon the theology
of justification as the critical basis of faith; on the other hand,
there is a corresponding emphasis upon the theology of sanctification. Faith cannot be alive without works. What is perfect
and inherent in Christ, as Hooker will put it, is not so in us

---

[17] ibid, p. 31.
[18] ibid, p. 42.

and yet it belongs to the Christian pilgrimage to endeavour to put on Christ. Christian faith is not static but dynamic; a dynamic that informs the patterns of prayer.

The teaching aspects of the Book of Common Prayer appear in the exhortations to Confession, to Communion, to the services of Baptism, and to Marriage and in the order of the services themselves. They reveal a pattern of theological understanding, rooted in Scripture and with a regard for the traditions of devotion belonging to the Western Church. There are a few important changes: a greater degree of clarity about sin and grace; shifts in the understanding of Christian marriage; and a greater degree of emphasis upon the individual in his or her appropriation of the principles of the Christian faith in a lively and personal manner. The liturgy of the Book of Common Prayer is never exactly *pro forma*; there is the constant appeal to the heart and mind of the individual soul.

The Exhortations have a wonderful explanatory force. They are part of the worship; even the Catechism is a service of worship. The experience of worship is more than something emotional; it is grounded in the feeling intellect, the mind that seeks after God. And there is the wonderful sense that there is something in worship for everyone, each according to the capacity of the beholder to behold. In short, there is the profound recognition about the nature of progression and regression in spiritual matters. It is one of the reasons for the form of General Confession and for the pattern of contrition, confession and satisfaction, that underlies the entire spiritual programme of the Book of Common Prayer.

The last poem in Herbert's *The Temple* is called *Love (III)*.[19] It captures the nature of that spiritual programme, moving from the soul's contrition, 'guiltie of dust and sinne', through confession, 'I, the unkinde, ungratefull', ultimately '[un]worthy to be here', to the redemptive grace of the Love of God which takes our hand and bids us 'sit down... and taste my meat'; in short, satisfaction. It reflects not only the dynamic of the

[19] Herbert, 'Love (III)', in *The Temple*, p. 180.

teaching conveyed in the exhortations but in the structure of the services themselves. There is the constant dialectic between justification and sanctification.

The minimalist aspect of the teaching is an important feature of the Book of Common Prayer. The Catechism emphasizes the necessity of knowing the Ten Commandments, the Creed and the Lord's Prayer. These basic instructions are not merely propositions but the living foundations of the soul's relation to God. In a way, the whole programme of prayer understands a certain relation between nature and grace. There is the sense of growing up into the life of Christ. The foundation is justifying grace; the process is sanctifying grace and the end is our glorification.

The Book of Common Prayer provides a critical education in the basic principles of the Christian faith as seen through the lenses of a modest but robust Reformed theology.

Language as Memory

The language of the Book of Common Prayer is memorable. As such it speaks to the faculty of memory in the soul. It was part of an educational programme, even the beginnings of a universal and public education, where every ploughboy (and girl) would be as well versed in the Scriptures as the most learned clerk at Oxford. A noble idea. The rhythms and refrains of the Prayer Book complement its doctrinal minimalism and inculcate a sense of spiritual identity and belonging.

In this sense, the Book of Common Prayer is more than a book. Through its language it becomes the spiritual *lingua franca* of a people, incorporating them into the community of God. Like the sermons of Lancelot Andrewes, which T. S. Eliot observed are known most for their strong lines of 'relevant intensity',[20] the Book of Common Prayer stands out for the quality of its memorable lines.

[20] T. S. Eliot, *For Lancelot Andrewes: Essays on Style and Order*, London: Faber (1970), p. 15.

The idea of ourselves as 'miserable sinners' for whom 'the remembrance of [our sins] is grievous unto us' and for whom 'the burden of our sins is intolerable', seems almost unthinkable if not altogether pathological and pathetic until we realize that what is described here is not about our emotional moods and feelings but an objective assessment of the human condition in the light of God's truth and mercy. We may never feel quite so intensely miserable, or then again, we may! But they are memorable.

There are such phrases as: 'we do not presume to come to this thy table trusting in our own righteousness'; the rich and symbolic phrase of our 'sacrifice of praise and thanksgiving'; the wonderful petitions and phrases in the Prayer for all Sorts and Conditions of Men and in the General Thanksgiving. The memorable aspect of the language of the Book of Common Prayer is one of the ways in which God lives in our souls through the mediation of language in which certain concepts and ideas remain within us.

P. D. James' novel, '*Devices and Desires*',[21] was published in 1989. She refused to countenance the provision of any explanation for the title, regarding it as the common property of any reasonably learned person to know its origin. It points to a marvellous confidence in the memorable qualities of great prose. And yet, the words of the General Confession are accessible and for all, and no phrase better captures us all in its net than the idea of 'the devices and desires of our hearts'.

Conclusion

Prayer, in George Herbert's poem, is expressed in a rich variety of images. There are images from scripture and theology, from the natural world and the domestic world, images of the exotic and the close at hand. His images of prayer reflect and extend a certain quality of the language of prayer in the Book of Common Prayer. It is at once intimate and transcendent. The poem offers an entire sequence of connected

[21] P. D. James (1989), *Devices and Desires*, London: Penguin Books.

images drawn from such a wide variety of sources, but it ends with the simple statement, 'something understood'.[22] Prayer is something understood in and through the ordered sequence of images.

George Herbert well understood the rhythms and patterns of the theological and prayerful language of the Book of Common Prayer. 'A kind of tune, which all things heare and feare,' he suggests, calling attention to its power to attract and arrest our attention, even as it opens us out to what is both close at hand and far away; 'Church-bels beyond the starres heard, the souls bloud'. The language of the Book of Common Prayer is about 'the soul in paraphrase, the heart in pilgrimage'. It is there for us to take up and make it our own.

It is 'something understood'.

---

[22] Herbert, 'Prayer (I)' in *The Temple*, p. 44.

The Prose and Poetry of the Book of Common Prayer

Ian Robinson

Ian Robinson was a pupil (and later editor) of F. R. Leavis and lectured for a long time at the University of Wales, Swansea, before becoming series editor of Edgeways Books. He has published on Chaucer and Chomsky, and a study of the evolution of modern English prose, Cranmer's Sentences, *as well as books in a genre he invented, 'criticism of language', beginning with* The Survival of English. *With Duke Maskell he is co-author of* The New Idea of a University. *He is a Trustee of the Prayer Book Society.*

It is generally recognized that the Book of Common Prayer is a very distinguished example of English prose. This traditional view is surely right; but it does not quite acknowledge the epoch-making originality of the Prayer Book.

Sometimes it is said that the English liturgists of the sixteenth century had an easy task because they had the good fortune to work in a great age of English prose. I shall give reasons for what may sound an extravagant opinion, that on the contrary, before the 1540s there was no English prose at all! – not, anyway, if we mean by 'prose' what has been meant since the 1660s: the ordinary non-verse form of the written language, in which thoughts are expressed in grammatically well-formed, often complex sentences. (Like that one, for instance, not this parenthesis without a finite verb.)

There is, of course, very good prose in Old English; in fact the English of the late Anglo-Saxon period were out of step with the rest of Western Christendom in establishing and using vernacular prose. King Alfred has as good a claim as anybody to have been the initiator of English prose, for the sorts of work where we still expect it, like deeds, laws and chronicles, as well as saints' lives and homilies. The Anglo-Saxon Chronicle, founded by that great king, was developed and kept going at a number of centres where there were some remarkable differences of opinion, emphasis, and eloquence; but all the versions were in prose, as we expect of ordinary prose, competently written by a number of not especially distinguished people. Homiletic prose could be better than that. The *Sermo Lupi ad Anglos* for instance is a powerful composition, and was possible to Bishop Wulfstan as a master of the non-verse spoken discourse working in a well-established tradition that survived the Conquest.

What never occurred before Cranmer was the now taken-for-granted union of prose with the syntax of the complex sentence.

My history master (more often than my English masters) would occasionally write in the margin of an essay, 'Not a sentence!' This was enough of a rebuke: there was no need to explain why sentences were required in essays (though not in marginalia, for 'not a sentence!' is not a sentence). It still surprises me, though I think I have established the fact, that the concept of 'sentence' in this schoolteachers' sense was not developed by grammarians before the seventeenth century, and that prose writers of the Middle Ages were not drilled to write in sentences. One essential of a modern sentence is that it ends with a full stop marking the limit of the domain of a finite verb. Before the sixteenth century punctuation, if any, was metrical and rhetorical, not syntactic. If a pause did not coincide with a syntactic boundary, whether of a clause or a sentence, the pause would be marked, not the syntactic boundary.

The *word* 'sentence', in Middle English and Early Modern English, meant, generally, 'meaning', as when Chaucer's Chanteclere misleads Pertelote about the 'sentence' of a Latin tag, or when Archbishop Cranmer, in a well-known letter to King Henry VIII apologising for his verses, says, 'As for the sentence, I suppose [it] will serve well enough'. In grammar, a sentence was 'a complete thought' and in rhetoric 'a memorable or weighty saying', as in the Funeral Sentences or the Sentences that precede Morning and Evening Prayer. The completeness of the thought was not recognized as, in the modern sense, the well-formedness of a sentence. A 'complete thought' could take part of a grammatical sentence or several grammatical sentences. The older senses survive in our adjective 'sententious' and in phrases like 'sentence of death', which has no syntactic implications unless the joining of head and body counts as syntax. (I have worked all this out to the best of my ability in my book *Cranmer's Sentences* to which I have to refer readers who want a fuller account.)

Winston Churchill found that the one reliable drill at Harrow was the writing of good English prose. 'I got into my bones,' says Churchill, 'the essential structure of the ordinary British sentence – which is a noble thing'.[1] Churchill's sentence could not have been understood in the time of Cranmer, because they would not have known what he meant by 'sentence'.

The next thing we take for granted about prose, after that it is written in sentences, is also there in Churchill's report: that prose is *ordinary*. In fact it may take a conscious effort to realize that prose is less natural than speech, though the common pattern is for civilisations to develop verse long before prose. Any modern educated person is expected to be able to write prose on demand, or at least was before they began examining history and other subjects by multiple-choice tick questions instead of by the writing of essays.

English prose was, of course, being used in the early sixteenth century for many of the purposes we expect of it, including the

---

[1] Winston S. Churchill (1930), *My Early Life: a Roving Commission*, p. 31.

first English outburst of printed pamphleteering (if the word 'pamphlet' is appropriate for works often hundreds of pages long with titles about as long as some modern pamphlets). This prose was not, however, in the complex but easy sentences we expect. Historically, fluent long sentences were more to be expected in verse; for instance the complex sentence, 29 lines long, at the beginning of *The Canterbury Tales*, would not have been attempted in prose, Chaucer's own prose not being particularly good. Ordinary English prose of the late Middle Ages was characteristically written in shortish phrases that might or might not be well-formed sentences.

With the onset of the Renascence the learned instinctively began to write English prose modelled on Latin. Much original English prose of the period in fact reads like a too literal translation. At the time they were aware of the danger of 'ink-horn terms', long words made out of Latin or Greek roots, but I have not come across anybody worried by the hopelessness of simply transferring Latin syntax into uninflected English. The reader frequently gets lost in sentences pages long, and which may or may not be ended with a full point. Stella Brook gives some examples, and remarks on the 'Chinese box arrangement of clauses within an imperfectly co-ordinated sentence' in a preface of William Caxton's, but I think her word 'breathless' is too kind.[2] Caxton was writing before the spring tide of Renascence Latinism, which got much worse. The technical term for much of this prose should be 'wandering'.

The educated English prose writers of the first 40 years of the sixteenth century are not breathless but long-winded. I do not exclude the exchanges between Tyndale and More, which I report as being (on both sides, by two writers of genius) full of sound and fury and pithy phrases, but now all but unreadable because there is no control of English sentence structure. Tyndale's genius comes out in the quite different prose of his

[2] Stella Brook (1965), *The Language of the Book of Common Prayer*, London, pp. 83, 84.

translations, More's in his Latin works and English speeches and narratives.

Then came the sudden demand for English prose to be used in the most important ways conceivable, for the Bible and the worship of God, and also for this prose to be ordinary, composed in large quantities by people of no special genius. How could it be done? (The Prayer Book is all in prose, even the ancient hymns and canticles, and the Psalm translation it uses is prose. Why this is so – why in England in the 1530s and 1540s verse was even less of a possibility than prose – is another story I hope to tell elsewhere.)

Bible prose was to some extent easier than Prayer Book prose, because Tyndale rightly followed the styles of the originals as closely as he could. Much of the narrative of the *koine* Greek of the New Testament is in short simple sentences, and by following that, Tyndale largely avoided the dangers of the wander. As to Biblical Hebrew, it must be one of the most paratactic languages in the world. (Parataxis is the repetition of simple forms, often joined by conjunctions, without co-ordination or subordination. In Hebrew, which is also sparing in its use of the verb to be, the previous sentence would have been put something like: '"parataxis" sayings pure and join sayings pure single: and not "co-ordinated" they and not "subordinate" they' – though I cannot guess what Jeremiah would have done for the grammatical terms.) There is hardly any subordination in Biblical Hebrew. Even if it makes any sense to think of the Old Testament as composed in sentences, which I do not believe, the vast majority of them begin with 'and' and (not counting the relative clauses beginning with the word-of-all-duty *asher* and the longish phrases telling who is speaking to whom, for which we use quotation marks) are about half a dozen words long. Tyndale's achievement was to do something comparable in real English.

So: modern English prose came in with the Prayer Book. It is surprising how far the discovery of how to write prose in English can be attributed to one time, and even to one person. Modern English prose was invented when Archbishop Cranmer worked out how to compose Collects.

The form of the Collect is not rigid, but there is a common layout. A petition, grammatically the main clause, is usually preceded by an invocation of one Person of the Trinity and a relative clause reminding us of one of his relevant attributes, then succeeded by an adverbial clause 'through Jesus Christ' or the like, and on great occasions ending with a doxology in another relative clause. The complete thought that is a Collect is therefore usually, in Latin, quite naturally one well-formed complex sentence. But *how to do this in English*? Stella Brook has a very good discussion of how Cranmer kept the basic principle of one Collect, one (modern) sentence, while using syntactic as well as rhythmic forms that belong to English not Latin.[3]

Another thing often said is that we were lucky in having had in Archbishop Thomas Cranmer a liturgist of unique genius. That is true of the basic grammar of the prayers only if it took genius to understand and do a necessary job of work which, in the nature of the case, had to be shared with many others. But it is not faint praise to notice that Cranmer, with no help from contemporary grammarians and rhetoricians, worked out the necessity of writing in (modern) sentences.

He did much more. Poetry is not restricted to verse; *poesis* is 'making' (from the same root as the first verb in the Septuagint, when God created heaven and earth), and much of the Prayer Book prose is poetry. The prose of the parts of the Prayer Book meant to be read aloud is, as generations of worshippers have confirmed, strong, clear, very good in poor acoustics, and often beautiful, with a functional beauty that comes from getting something well said.

Here Cranmer was not without a tradition to work in, the one I have mentioned, going back to Ælfric and Wulfstan.

---

[3] Brook, op. cit., pp. 131 ff. Dr Brook, before the days of *Common Worship*, found it necessary to defend the Collects themselves against charges of wordiness and wandering!

Amongst the rhetorical devices of Prayer Book prose the most obvious is repetition. This goes deep into the habit of the language, often along with alliteration, as in 'kith and kin', 'time and tide'. Bear in mind that for 1000 years or so the most ordinary English verse was in two-beat alliterative phrases where repetition and slight variation was endemic.

Rhythm is of the utmost importance. Rhythm is still sometimes confused with metre, but is of the essence of prose too. What one means by speech rhythm or prose rhythm is not as straightforward as it may seem, but phrases built round beats or stresses to which lesser stresses are related are obviously important, as is also what I call 'rhythmic contour', often involving intonation, which will give a shape to a whole clause or sentence.

In this limited space I will draw attention only to the two most noticeable patterns of prose rhythm in the Prayer Book, which at the risk of coining technical terms I will call type 1 and type 2. Type 1 is the longer phrase made of two two-beat phrases, a shape taken over from alliterative verse but ending with a bang. The immemorial custom of alliterative verses, similarly made out of two halves each of two beats, was to end with an unstressed syllable. This from the Benedicite has a rhythmic structure much like that of a line of Piers Plowman but without alliteration and ending with a stress, 'O ye Sun, and Moon, bless ye the Lord'. Unsurprisingly all the words are monosyllables.

Type 2, not quite as frequent, is the phrase also made of two two-beat smaller phrases but ending with a cadence in cursus form, that is, one of a small set of rhythmic patterns which all end with either one or two unstressed syllables. Characteristically the cadenced form will complete a prose verse that began with a type-1 phrase ending in a beat.

The very ancient cadences expected at the ends of phrases in both verse and prose, were codified by the medieval papacy. In English there are three, with recognisable stress-patterns for the last seven, six or five syllables of a phrase. The verbs that may be expected to end a classical Latin period most often end with a short syllable. English, as well as depending more on stress than length, tends not to put the verb at the end, and to have more words not ending in a stress, so cadences do not come so easily. But there are enough sentences in the Prayer Book that end with English cursus forms to show that the composers wrote these patterns either deliberately or instinctively.

In the Benedicite, for instance, the predominantly type-1 phrases like the one just quoted are balanced in a complete verse by the type-2 chorus line which is repeated 32 times.

> O ye Sun, and Moon, bless ye the Lord: praise him, and magnify him for ever.
> O ye Stars of Heaven, bless ye the Lord: praise him, and magnify him for ever.

and so on. The first half of both these verses is made of two two-beat smaller phrases, ending with the main stress of the phrase, with beats on *sun, moon, bless* and *Lord* in the first, *Stars, Heaven, bless* and *Lord* in the second. Then the chorus phrase is also made out of four beats (allowing the second *him* to take a beat) but ending with the falling rhythm of a velox, the scarcest of the three cursus forms – dactyl followed by two trochees, in English túm te te túm te túm te. This phrase is actually enriched by an extra preceding dactyl, so that the whole pattern is two dactyls followed by two trochees, túm te te túm te te túm te túm te.

The Benedicite is very far from a one-off in the Prayer Book, the Psalter and the Bible. Something very similar happens in Psalm 136, with the chorus line 'for his mercy endureth for ever' ending with the commonest cursus form, the planus, túm te te túm te, also enriched by another preceding dactyl, the phrase balancing the first half of a 'sentence' that is often though not always made out of a type-1 formation of two two-beat phrases ending with a beat:

> The moon and the stars to govern the night
> For his mercy endureth for ever ...

Yea, and slew mighty kings
For his mercy endureth for ever ...
Who divided the Red Sea in two parts
For his mercy endureth for ever

and so on.

The responses to the first nine Commandments end iambic, with a stress '... to keep this law', but for the tenth we have another enriched planus, '... laws in our hearts, we beseech thee', two dactyls and trochee. 'Father Almighty', the end of the first paragraph of the Gloria in Excelsis, is another planus, túm te te túm te. What reason apart from making a cursus could there be for this ending rather than 'Almighty Father'? Then:

Thou that takest away the sins of the world / have mercy upon us.

Here two two-beat phrases ending in a beat are followed by a phrase (in this case of only two beats) ending in a cadence, for *mercy upon us*, túm te te túm te, is another planus, in this short hymn repeated three times. In the following Blessing, 'all understanding' and 'remain with you always' are further instances of planus. This last could have been 'always remain with you', but that would lose the cadence. Of course similar rhythmic shapes are frequent in the English Bible, as 'And all thy children shall be taught of the Lord, and great shall be the peace of thy children' (Isa. 54.13): a two two-beat phase ending with a beat followed by a two two-beat phrase ending with a planus.

These forms are not restricted to the end of syntactic sentences. For instance the Collect for the First Sunday in Advent, poetry if there is poetry in English! comes to a climax before the 'through' clause with 'rise to the life immortal', a velox, túm te te túm te túm te. The use of cadence forms is still prose not verse, rhythmic but not metrical, and there is no irregularity if these shapes are not made, so it is a serious illiteracy when *Common Worship* prints Prayer Book passages as verse; it damages reading by suggesting that we should make metrical patterns.

If rhetoric becomes automatic it fails; all depends, with these figures of sound, on what the composer makes of them, just as in verse everything depends on what a poet does with metre. Stella Brook finds an unusual case of 'thoroughly clumsy syntax' in the second Collect at Evening Prayer: '... that both ... and also, that we being by thee defended ...'.[4] Well, this does need a pause after 'both', which should not be too hard for the minister. But listen to the prayer well intoned by a single voice in a big stone building and you will hear why Cranmer did not resist the rhyme/assonance of 'we being by thee ...'.

Genuine rhetoric properly handled *makes* what would otherwise be less forceful or not expressed at all. Here perhaps the word 'genius' can really be applied to Cranmer. He has a wonderful sense of *tempo*, of what needs slowing and emphasis. This is the reason for some of the repetitions which any modern sub-editor would delete. There is no difference between erring and straying. What is the difference between 'declare' and 'pronounce'? Devices are not quite the same as desires, but the sub-editor would think the expansion unnecessary. At these places in the Confession and Absolution at Morning and Evening Prayer the repetitions slow the pace and emphasize something we should momentarily dwell on.

The prayers *not* meant to be said by the congregation do not go so well when they are; e.g. the Prayer of Humble Access is composed for a single voice that has an intimacy lost when the whole congregation join in with voice as well as spirit. Conversely, the prayers we all join in are carefully phrased (helped by the typographical device of starting a new breath-phrase, which need not be a sentence, with a capital) so as to allow the congregation good simple rhythmic shapes.

There are two observations to be made in support of the thesis that the Prayer Book brought in modern English prose,

[4] Brook, op. cit., p. 135.

not ordinarily expected to be read aloud, as well as perfecting the prose of public oratory. The first is that Cranmer, as presiding influence, learned his own lesson beyond the parts of the Prayer Book meant to be read aloud: there are the rubrics and the prefaces. They are all well and clearly written in modern prose. Moreover Cranmer's own writing both in letters and in the Preface to the Great Bible and the *Defence of the True and Catholic Doctrine of the Sacrament* is very good English prose. The second edition of the *Defence* incorporated the objections of Bishop Stephen Gardiner. To see the difference between the Renascence wander and good modern prose, read any of Gardiner's animadversions then Cranmer's reply.

The other sign that the Prayer Book brought in a new prose was that the style became established as ordinary for liturgical work, though it did not immediately catch on universally, for the wander continued. Of the two books of Homilies the first, edited by Cranmer, is in far better prose than the second. Hooker, the central theologian of the Church of England, wrote prose which Cranmer would never have let go.

Once the style is made, though, others can use it. Would anyone know without being told that Cosin's Collect for Advent 3 is not by the same author as Cranmer's for Advent 1? And the tinkerings with the Prayer for the Church Militant ended up in 1662 with the remembrance of those departed this life which, again, nobody would from the style recognize as an addition. From Cranmer's day to ours countless occasional prayers have been and are made fluently in the Prayer Book style.

The Prayer Book took hold of the nation – compulsorily. *Everybody* had to go to church, and for longer than is now the custom, for the ordinary Sunday morning pattern was Morning Prayer, Litany and Ante-Communion with sermon.

Modern English prose definitively replaced the old wander in the same decade as the re-establishment of the Book of Common Prayer. In the decade of the Restoration secular prose as we know it was firmly established by Dryden and his friends, much influenced by Cranmer. For the next 300 and more years, the Prayer Book was always a sort of presupposition of ordinary prose, a guarantee of the effectiveness of our ordinary way of making sense, and a guarantee that the language, the national mind, is not altogether godless or trivial.

In the successor situation in which we live no new character has developed in Church or Nation, but the character of both has become shadowy, without definition. The deposition of the Prayer Book, along with the loss of the English Bible, is not distinguishable from the disunification of England. The reunification may yet find its model in 1662.

For Further Reading

Stella Brook (1965), *The Language of the Book of Common Prayer,* London.

R. W. Chambers (1932), *On the Continuity of English Prose from Alfred to More and his School,* Oxford [Early English Text Society].

C. S. Lewis (1944), *English Literature in the Sixteenth Century, excluding Drama,* Oxford.

Catherine Pickstock (1998), *After Writing: on the Liturgical Consummation of Philosophy,* Oxford.

Ian Robinson (2003), *Cranmer's Sentences,* Denton (originally published 1998 as *The Establishment of Modern English Prose in the Reformation and the Enlightenment,* Cambridge).

Timothy Rosendale (2007), *Liturgy and Literature in the Making of Protestant England,* Cambridge.

Ramie Targoff (2001), *Common Prayer: the Language of Public Devotion in Early Modern England,* Chicago.

Peter Toon & Louis R. Tarsitano (2003, revised 2004), *Neither Archaic nor Obsolete: The Language of Common Prayer and Public Worship,* Denton.

Section 3

Worshipping with the Book of Common Prayer

Like Eagles in this Life:
A Theological Reflection
on 'The Order for the
Administration of the Lord's
Supper or Holy Communion'
in the Prayer Books of 1559
and 1662[1]

Gavin Dunbar

The Revd Gavin Dunbar was born in Toronto, Canada, and educated at Trinity College, Toronto; Dalhousie University, Halifax; and Wycliffe College, Toronto. He was ordained a priest in the diocese of Nova Scotia in 1992 and has been rector of St. John's Church in Savannah, Georgia, since 2006. He is currently President of the Prayer Book Society of the United States of America.

[1] This essay is dedicated with affection and gratitude to the memory of Fr Robert Crouse, who died at home in Crousetown, Nova Scotia, on 14 January 2011. Earlier versions of this paper were delivered at the Atlantic Theological Conference in Moncton, New Brunswick, in June 2010, and also in Savannah, Thomasville, and Oklahoma City. My thanks especially to Fr Gary Thorne, Drew Nathaniel Keane, and Prudence Dailey for their invaluable suggestions and criticisms.

When the sixteenth-century English Reformers thought
about the conditions upon which man's communion with God
in Christ is established and sustained, they spoke in terms of
the work of grace both outward and inward. Outwardly,
God's grace is manifest in his incarnate Son's death upon
the cross, the Righteous One's suffering for sinners, and in
the Church's dissemination of the Gospel, in the ministry of
Word and Sacrament. Inwardly, God's grace elicits a triad of
human responses whereby the grace revealed in Christ, and
in the Gospel, is appropriated: repentance, faith, and those
good works (especially those of love), done in obedience to
the Commandments, which are the fruits of a living faith,
and which testify to gratitude for this grace.[2] The outward
grace is the activity of the divine Word; the inward grace is
the activity of the divine Spirit. What the Word signifies, the
Spirit effects: together they accomplish the Father's eternal
purpose.

This understanding of man's communion with God,
grounded upon the doctrines of Christ and of grace formulated
by the ancient Catholic church,[3] found liturgical expression in

---

[2] To illustrate this threefold inward grace from Scripture, one might consider
a passage like that of the penitent thief, Lk. 23.39–43. The thief enters into
communion with God – with Christ in Paradise, as Christ tells him – after he
responds to other malefactor's gibe at Jesus ('If thou be Christ, save thyself
and us' 23.39) with *repentance* ('dost thou not fear God, seeing thou art in
the same condemnation, and we indeed justly; for we receive the due reward
of our deeds' 23.40, 41); with *faith* that recognizes Christ's righteousness
('this man hath done nothing amiss' Lk. 23.41); and in the prayer that is
one of the chief *good works* of fruitful faith ('Lord, remember me when thou
comest into thy kingdom' 23.42). The outward grace of the Word of God
eliciting this inward grace is indicated in 24.46–47: 'Thus it behoved Christ
to suffer, and to rise from the dead the third day: and that repentance and
remission of sins should be preached in his name among all nations'.

[3] The influence of Augustine's doctrine on the reformers is often noted. The
influence of the Christology of Chalcedon upon the reformed consensus
on justification and sanctification is also important. See for instance,
W. J. Torrance Kirby (2005), 'Christ and the Church: a "Chalcedonian"
Ecclesiology', pp. 79–96 in *Richard Hooker, Reformer and Platonist*.

the Eucharistic rite devised by Thomas Cranmer on the basis of the ancient Latin Mass of the western church, revised and translated into English both memorable and convincing. 'The Order of the Administration of the Lord's Supper or Holy Communion' published in the English Prayer Book of 1549, and further revised in 1552, has twice suffered eclipse and twice been revived, once, after a 'papist' reaction, in 1559, and then, after a 'puritan' revolution, in 1662. It is once again in eclipse: but perhaps its present neglect is the condition for the rediscovery of its merits.

The triad of repentance, faith, and works, is, as J. I. Packer has observed, the fundamental building block of Cranmer's liturgy.[4] By the mid-sixteenth century, this triad was a commonplace of Protestant orthodoxy.[5] Cranmer's accomplishment was to rethink the Church's ancient liturgy in light of this understanding. However one may regret the severity of the sixteenth-century iconoclasm – a steep price to pray for reform – Cranmer's work was a genuine advance, re-presenting the ancient tradition for the new-born modern world with a renewed clarity of theological understanding.

---

[4] Packer used the terms 'sin, grace, faith', although the reference for his analysis I have not been able to locate.

[5] Commenting on the similar structural triad of 'guilt, grace, and gratitude' in the Heidelberg Catechism of 1562, Lyle D. Bierma traces it to Luther's reading of the Epistle to the Romans, as mediated by Melanchthon's own treatise, the *Loci Communes Theologici* of 1521, for which it supplied the overall structure. He notes, however, that 'By the mid-sixteenth century, the triad of law–gospel–good works or sin–faith–love had become so much a part of the common stock of Protestant theology that the threefold division of the [Heidelberg Catechism] cannot be traced with any certainty to a particular source of author.' (Lyle D. Bierma et al. (2005), *An introduction to the Heidelberg Catechism: sources, history, and theology*, p. 86.) In the Prayer Book liturgy, a similar triad appears (in the Catechism of 1549 and in the Baptismal rite of 1662) in the threefold baptismal vow, to renounce, believe, and obey. Only the first two vows, to renounce and to believe, appear in the pre-Reformation Latin rites of baptism, although the idea of obedience is not far away.

Yet to comprehend Cranmer's art, one must also attend to the observation of Rowan Williams,[6] that Cranmer does not lay out his ideas in the linear fashion often found in recent liturgies, but is content to revisit themes already touched on, in a fashion which has sometimes provoked criticism. The result, as Williams points out, is a kind of spiral movement (not unknown in other works, such as the Gospel of John), so that one returns to similar ideas, but from a different angle, in a different context, recapitulating what has already been said but also revealing something new. The effect on the worshipper of this cyclical spiral motion is profound. Each return to the idea reinforces it, while at the same time allowing it to be expanded and deepened.[7]

The question is, of course, what this recapitulation means, and where this spiral leads. To the *triad* observed by Packer and the *spiral* observed by Williams we turn to Cranmer himself for the third idea, which is that of *ascent* into heavenly places:

> ... being like eagles in this life, we should fly up into heaven in our hearts, where that Lamb is resident at the right hand of his Father, which taketh away the sins of the world; by whose stripes we are made whole; by whose passion we are filled at his table; and whose blood we receiving out of his holy side, do live for ever ....[8]

The spiral ascent of the eagle in repentance, faith, and love, has an end that is endless. It draws us up into Christ crucified, risen, and glorified, into participation in the divine nature, into the inner life of the Trinity. Somewhat paradoxically, therefore, in

[6] In his sermon on the 450th anniversary of Cranmer's martyrdom, Tuesday 21 March 2006 given at the invitation of the Prayer Book Society, at St Mary the Virgin, Oxford. The full text may be found at: http://www.archbishopof-canterbury.org/353
[7] The benefits of such recapitulation are being rediscovered by educators.
[8] From the 'Disputations at Oxford' in *Writings and Disputations of Thomas Cranmer ... relative to the Lord's Supper*, edited for the Parker Society by the Rev. John Edmund Cox, M. A. (1844), p. 398.

our ascent we come to the ground of the Church, in the end to our beginning. The holy city, new Jerusalem, as St John observes, is seen coming down from God out of heaven (Rev. 21.2).

Preparatory Prayers

It is one of the marks of Cranmer's Liturgy that he likes to begin from the Lord's Prayer. In this way he signals that the Church's worship takes its beginning not from itself but from Christ, and his teaching. It is only through Christ that we have access to the Father in prayer, and it is in obedience to his teaching that we learn to pray. In doing so, we make our own the priorities of the Son, namely the Father's glory and goodness. As the Son is entirely oriented in heart and mind towards the Father, so his disciples must be also, in devotion to his glory, and in dependence upon his grace.

The Lord's Prayer is followed by another ancient text, the Collect for Purity, a kind of *epiclesis* (or invocation of the Spirit) 'to cleanse the thoughts of our hearts ... that we may perfectly love thee and worthily magnify thy holy name'. If the Word of God in the Lord's Prayer sets out the chief end of worship as the hallowing of the Father's Name, in the Collect for Purity we seek the purifying grace of the Spirit as the chief means by which we may 'love' and 'magnify' the name of God in accordance with his Word.[9] Our aim is to worship the Father in Spirit and in Truth.

These preparatory prayers set before us the essential nature of worship, its end and its means. The worship of God is not the means to another end in this world, but is the end in itself. As the Westminster Catechism so memorably put it, 'man's chief end is to glorify God and to enjoy him for ever'. The conversion of mankind, and the liberation of the world

---

[9] Purity of heart, as Kierkegaard famously defined it, 'is to will one thing' – the one pure and perfect good, which is God. The intellectualist language of 'thoughts' in this ancient Collect is scriptural, of course (Gen. 6.5; Lk. 2.35, Heb. 4.12), but also a legacy of the Desert Fathers as transmitted by the writings of Evagrius and Cassian about the 'thoughts' (*logismoi*) of the heart.

(the ends of much contemporary liturgy), are futile unless the worship of God is their end. The primary orientation of the community at worship is Godward. It is as we seek first the hallowing of the Father's name, the coming of his Kingdom and the doing of his will, that we may expect daily bread, forgiveness of sins, and deliverance from evil.

If the preparatory prayers indicate that the fundamental orientation of the community at worship is toward God, they also indicate that the means by which this is accomplished, is his Word and Spirit. Only as we begin from God, in his Son, and continue in him, in his Spirit, can we attain to him, as Father. The Church's worship is thus a divine work: it is God knowing himself, and loving himself, through the Church.[10] Everything in worship is subordinated to this movement of spirit, of mind and will, through God toward God, and the Collect draws attention to the invisible and inward dimension of the Liturgy, addressing the God 'unto whom all hearts are open, all desires known and from whom no secrets are hid'; and asking that he 'cleanse the thoughts of our hearts'. It is thus no surprise that the logic of the service from this point on is dictated chiefly by the exercise of three virtues in their logical sequence: repentance, faith, and works. The governing 'shape of the liturgy' is not an external action but the spiritual logic of Communion, the conditions of human participation in the divine life.

Ante-Communion

From the preparatory prayers we pass to the first of three triads of repentance, faith, and works, in the first great division of the Lord's Supper that is known as the Ante-Communion, the service that precedes the Communion itself.[11]

---

[10] A theme to which the service returns in the Blessing which concludes it.

[11] Up until the later nineteenth century, the Ante-Communion could and often did stand on its own, as well as serving as a general preparation for the Communion.

The Law

The Ante-Communion begins with the rehearsal of the Ten Commandments – no novelty to the Catholic tradition, as the catechetical addresses of Thomas Aquinas indicate – in which the faithful learn that the right worship of God (set forth in the first four Commandments) for which they have just prayed involves also the fulfillment of the obligations of righteousness toward their neighbours (set forth in the last six Commandments). Following the precedent of the Scottish Prayer Book, the Decalogue is often replaced by the Summary of the Law, which teaches us to interpret the law in terms of charity. Yet the Decalogue brings before us the requirements of righteousness in our actual human community; whereas modern Christians find it easy to dissolve charity into vague sentiment. Fellowship in holiness with the Lord will require a right relation with man as well as God, obedient action not just easy feeling. This knowledge of the righteousness required by God moves us first to repentance ('Lord, have mercy upon us', the law as the ministry of condemnation, awakening our hearts to sin) but also to hope in God's grace ('incline our hearts to keep this law', the law as pattern of righteousness).

The Collects

It is not in us to fulfil the righteousness required by the Law; it is the gift of God, and this gift of grace must be asked for. This desire for grace, stirred up by the rehearsal of the Law, finds expression in the Collect which follows, one for each Sunday and holy day in the year. They are *petitions*. 'The Church approaches God in all that indigence and need that must be a part of her in this earthly pilgrimage'.[12] In the balanced antitheses of ancient rhetorical art, the Collects – which largely originate in the Roman church of late antiquity under the influence of Augustine's doctrine

[12] Jungmann, Joseph A. (1951), *The Mass of the Roman Rite: its origins and development*, I, p. 378.

of grace[13] – teach us to look with confident expectation to the greatness of the Father's power and goodness to relieve the need of man, a confidence grounded upon sure trust in Christ, whose mediation prevails because he as Son and Lord 'liveth and reigneth' with the Father 'in the unity of the Holy Ghost, ever one God, world without end'.[14]

The Lessons, Creed, and Sermon

With the Epistle, Gospel, Creed, Sermon and Notices, we pass to the moment of Faith which hears and receives the divine word of grace revealed in Christ, preached by the Apostles, confessed in the Creeds, explained and applied by the Clergy. We are guided into a right faith and understanding of the Word of God in three ways: first, by the doctrinal logic of the ancient Eucharistic lectionary of the Western church – a legacy of great value, sadly dismissed and neglected in our time;[15] second, by

---

[13] The Collect of the day is accompanied by one of two Collects for the monarch, one asking for his people's obedience, the other looking for his obedience to God. The appearance of the Christian prince at this point in the liturgy, 'knowing whose minister he is', who seeks God's honour and glory, and his people's welfare, whom the people are in conscience bound to serve and obey, indicates the very public nature of the community which is being established in the liturgy. It is not a sect, gathered against the larger society outside: but the larger Christian society in its ecclesiastical aspect. The inward movement of Spirit of grace and the outward life of institutions though distinct, are not separate, and are interwoven in constant dialectic. The late modern secularization of civil society presents a particular challenge to the Church at this point.

[14] The editing of the conclusion of the collects in the 1662 Prayer Book is one its chief defects. The sixteenth-century Prayer Books clearly expect the priest to supply the full Trinitarian ending to the Collect of the day.

[15] The chief feature of the ancient lectionary – retained more fully by the Lutheran and Anglican reformers than by the Tridentine Missal! – is the provision of a coherent doctrinal teaching for each Sunday and other holy days, keyed to the logic of the Church's year. While the late twentieth century lectionaries – the *Ordo Lectionum Missae* (1970), and its successors, the *Common Lectionary*, and *Revised Common Lectionary* (RCL) – offer a greater quantity of Scripture (three lessons and psalmody in a three-year cycle), they do so at the cost of doctrinal coherence, not only in the 'ordinary

the ancient catholic creed of Nicea; and third, by the sermon
delivered (at least notionally!) by a learned and eloquent
preacher ordained and licensed by ecclesiastical authority.
Here is no private reading of Scripture, no unmediated access
to the Word of God, but one taught by the Church in fidelity
to the historic Faith. Notably it is in the ancient, ecumenical,
corporate, ecclesial, and dogmatic formulation of the Nicene
Creed that the personal faith of the individual Christian finds
expression. What 'I believe' is not some vagary of subjective
fancy, but what has been believed 'by everyone, in every place,
at every time'. Personal faith is not blown about by every wind
of doctrine, but finds itself anchored in what Hooker called
'ancient continuance'; and individual faith becomes a point of
continuity with the past, not an occasion for radical disruption
and re-invention. Only in the context of the *Church's* faith and
worship is the Word of God rightly preached and received.

Yet having rendered due acknowledgment to the ecclesial
aspect of the Word of God, one must acknowledge that it
is the Word of *God* that is proclaimed and received, not the
Word of the Church. Though the revelation be entrusted to
the Church, what elicits and shapes the Faith of the Church is
the revelation of God in Christ, set forth in the Scriptures. In
this revelation we move beyond what finite, worldly wisdom
deems conceivable or possible, to embrace an infinite wisdom.
In the Word of God, a new and heavenly standpoint is revealed
for man, a new beginning point for knowledge, understanding,
discernment, decision and expectation (Rev. 4.1).

The Offertory
The third moment in the triad of conversion, the exercise of good
works, especially those of charity, encourages a communion of
goods both spiritual and material. This 'faith active in love'

time' where (in the RCL) the three lessons have *in principle* no connection
with each other, but also in the 'special' seasons like Lent, when the increased
quantity of Scripture comes at the expense of doctrinal clarity. It is heartening
to see a recovery of the older lectionary by younger Lutheran and Anglican
clergy, often in defiance of received opinion.

(Gal. 5.6) begins appropriately in a compendium of scriptural texts, moving us to give alms and oblations for the relief of the poor and the support of the clergy. It is also scriptural teaching 'by thy holy Apostle' (a reference to 1 Tim. 2.1) that moves us to prayer 'for the whole state of Christ's Church militant here in earth', a prayer universal in its scope, embracing 'all those who do confess thy holy Name'. As Charles Wheatley notes, 'our alms perhaps are confined to a few indigent neighbours; but our prayers may extend to all mankind, by recommending them all to the mercies of God, who is able to relieve them all'.[16] This prayer makes explicit the catholic scope of Christian charity, the reality that Christian prayer is always prayer for the whole number of those who are chosen in Christ.

Its object is sharply focused: it is a prayer for the *Church*: that is, for the community of the redeemed called into existence by the Word of God. In modern liturgies, Christians are invited to pray 'for the needs of the church and of the world', a formulation that all sides of the sixteenth-century Reformation would have found theologically and biblically strange.[17] *Extra ecclesiam nulla salus* ('No Salvation outside the Church') was the doctrine of the Reformers as well as the Fathers: as Calvin says, echoing St Cyprian of Carthage, 'he who refuses to be a son of the Church desires in vain to have God as his Father'.[18] For the Reformers, as throughout the Christian tradition, 'the world' refers (at best) to unredeemed human society, and (very often) to one of the 'three foes of man' from whose bondage we are delivered by Christ.[19] The

---

[16] Charles Wheatley (1858), *A rational illustration of the Book of Common Prayer*, Cambridge, p. 326. Here as elsewhere Wheatley's work (first published 1710) is abbreviating material from *A Companion to the Temple* (1672–6) by Thomas Comber (1645–1699, Dean of Durham from 1691).

[17] Compare the 'high priestly' prayer of Jn 17.9, in which Christ prays '*not* for the world, but for them which thou hast given me', the Church.

[18] *Commentary on the Epistle to the Galatians*, p. 88.

[19] Compare the first vow of baptism, to renounce 'the devil and all his works, the vain pomp and glory of the world, with all covetous desires of the same, and the carnal desires of the flesh.'

grace of Christ claimed in the Lord's Supper is the grace of the New Testament promised and covenanted to his Church, not to the world in its enmity to him and his purposes. However inclusive in its catholic universality, the Prayer for the Church remains firmly rooted in the catholic truth of the revelation of God in Christ.

The Prayer begins with a petition to inspire 'the universal church with the spirit of truth, unity, and concord', and the order of those nouns is significant. Unity follows upon a common knowledge of the truth and produces a mutual willing of the good: 'Grant that all they that do confess thy holy name, may agree in the truth of thy holy word, and live in unity and godly love'. Apart from orthodoxy in belief, therefore, we have no true community. 'Doctrine divides' has been one of the most divisive mantras of our current controversies. Assuming the opposition of doctrine and unity, the adherents of unity have abandoned doctrine, and the adherents of doctrine have abandoned unity. We must reject this polarization as contrary to the Trinitarian faith: for the Spirit, the unitive bond of love, is of one substance with the Son, who is the Word of God's truth. As in the Trinity, so in the Church: though Word and Spirit, mind and will, knowledge and love, truth and unity, are co-equal and co-inherent, there is a logical order to them. Truth has a unitive power; unity fulfils truth.

After the doctrine of the Church's spiritual unity presented in the first paragraph of the Prayer for the Church, the middle paragraphs address the institutional structures through which this unity is realized – the Christian prince and magistrate, the Christian pastor, together governing the Christian people. We pray for the king and council, and for nobles and magistrates serving under his authority, that they may 'truly and indifferently administer justice, to the punishment of wickedness and vice, and to the maintenance of God's true religion and virtue'. We pray for clergy that they may set 'forth thy true and lively word' and 'rightly and duly administer thy holy Sacraments'. And we pray for the people, that 'with meek heart and due reverence they may hear and receive thy holy word, truly serving thee in holiness and righteousness all the days of their life'. The word of God exerts its authority on the whole of society in its civil and ecclesiastical aspects.

After institutions, we pray for those in adversity, including those whom our alms have sought to relieve, whom we commend to God's comfort and succour. The Church is defined not just by institutions of power but also by its solidarity with those who suffer. The 'comfort' for which we somewhat tersely pray is spelled out more fully in the Visitation of the Sick in terms of the patience and repentance whereby we attain conformity with Christ: 'who went not up to joy, but first he suffered pain, and entered not in glory, before he was crucified. So truly our way to eternal life is to suffer here with Christ, and our door to enter into eternal life is gladly to die with Christ, that we may rise again from death, and dwell with him in everlasting life'. As a later prayer says, through 'patience under their sufferings' (carrying the cross), they come to 'a happy issue from all their afflictions' (resurrection).[20]

That the prayer for those who suffer holds back from stating more fully the mystery of their participation in the cross and resurrection, indicates that in the order of the Lord's Supper, the moment for this has not yet fully come. What Cranmer does not (yet) say is as important as what he does. In the prayer for the Church we begin to see the communion of God with man in Christ, proclaimed by the Word of God, anticipated in the faith that works by love: but there is yet more to be seen.

Second Cycle – Immediate Preparation for Communion
At this point in the service, we have attained a certain completeness: a Church constituted by the Word of God in

[20] The Prayer 'for All Sorts and Conditions of Men', perhaps composed by Dr Gunning, later Bishop of Chichester and Ely, who took part in the Savoy Conference that led to the 1662 Prayer Book. This 'happy issue' was acknowledged more fully in the 1662 remembrance of the faithful departed, and its petition for our share with them in the kingdom of heaven.

repentance, in faith, in love. We have made a beginning: and yet, paradoxically, we have not yet come to the true beginning, the ground and principle of the Church. A further ascent is required. At this point, therefore, a new cycle of acts of repentance, faith, and charity begins, which is introduced by one of three Exhortations and an Invitation to Communion, and consists in the Confession, whereby we are exercised in repentance; the Absolution and Comfortable Words, exercising our faith; and the *Sursum corda* ('Lift up your hearts'), Preface ('It is very meet, right, and our bounden duty'), and *Sanctus* ('Holy, Holy, Holy'), exercising us in charity with the heavenly city in giving thanks and praise to God.

We begin with two points about this middle cycle. First, while the Ante-Communion provided a general preparation, at no point was the Sacrament itself mentioned.[21] No doubt this allowed for the possibility of the Ante-Communion as a service in itself, but it also contributes to the sense of greater things held in reserve. Now, in the Exhortations, the Sacrament comes explicitly into view, with its requirement of our separation from sin by means of repentance and amendment of life, and our reconciliation to God and our neighbours in charity. The Exhortations and the Confession set out the three dimensions of repentance in confession and contrition ('we acknowledge ... our manifold sins and wicked-nesses' in confession and we 'bewail' them in contrition) but also satisfaction. We are to make restitution for harm done and seek reconciliation with estranged neighbours, and if our sins are open and notorious, the curate himself is to admonish and if necessary repel us from the holy Table (so the opening rubrics). There is no disconnect between the sacramental and the social.

Second, though rooted firmly in the concrete actuality of human society, in this second cycle we turn both inwards and

---

[21] There was one petition referring to it in the 1549 Prayer for the Church, but it did not survive the Prayer's migration to its concluding position in the 1552 Ante-Communion.

upwards, in a kind of dialectic. On the one hand, we descend into the soul, into its alienation from God, confronting the gravity of our sins, and looking to God to overcome the distance from him which our sins have caused. On the other hand, when he does so, and looses us from the bondage and burden of our sins, we rise buoyantly and spontaneously towards him, we 'lift up our hearts to the Lord' in praise and thanksgiving, we join 'with angels and archangels and all the company of heaven' in adoration of the most Holy.[22] What comes between, translating sinners into sanctity, is the Absolution and Comfortable Words, in which the mercy of God, and the saving mediation of Christ, is declared for faith to receive. Though the General Confession, and the *Sursum Corda*, Preface, and *Sanctus* are all ancient elements from the pre-Reformation Liturgy,[23] the movement in this second cycle

---

[22] In the Platonism of ancient Christianity, the development of the theme of angelic worship in the Preface presumably reflects an understanding of faith's ascent from things corporeal to things incorporeal and intelligible, on its way to the supreme Good. It is striking that this perspective is not abandoned by Protestant reformers like Cranmer and Calvin, who will refer to worship as entering into the presence of God and the holy angels (e.g. *Institutes* III. iv.11: 'in every sacred assembly we stand before the sight of our God and the angels'.

[23] In *The Mass According to the Roman Rite: its origins and development* (1949, trans. 1950), Joseph Jungmann notes that from the ninth century through the rest of the Middle Ages the Latin Rite's provision for Epistle, Gospel, and Creed, was often supplemented after the sermon by notices, general intercessions, and, at least in German churches, a General Confession based on the *Confiteor* – all or mainly in the vernacular (Volume I, 480–494). He does not give evidence of the practice of a General Confession in English Rites (though the Prone or Bidding Prayer is known to have supplied the place of a General Intercession), but even if a vernacular General Confession was not a feature of the English Rites, Cranmer might well have known of the custom from his extensive contacts with German Lutherans, and his study of Lutheran liturgical practice, which was highly conservative in all things indifferent. If so, here as elsewhere (notably the daily office lectionary), precisely at the moment where Cranmer seems most obviously 'Reformed', he is in fact building on long-established Catholic tradition, according to the conservative and traditional principle that Hooker dubbed 'ancient continuance'.

corresponds to the archetypal reformed logic of 'guilt, grace, and gratitude'. If the first cycle represents the Church of the Word of God, this second cycle represents the Church as the company of earthly sinners and heavenly saints – *simul justus et peccator*, sinner and righteous all at once.

In the Comfortable Words – sometimes accused of undermining the assurance of forgiveness expressed in the Absolution – we see the very ground and basis of the loosing from the bonds of sin which the Absolution authoritatively declares: the authority of 'Christ Jesus', which is the authority of God's saving love, who 'came into the world to save sinners'; 'Jesus Christ the righteous', who is even now in the heavenly places our 'advocate with the Father', and the 'propitiation for our sins'. The principal moments of the Son's coming forth from and return to the Father indicated in the Comfortable Words, are specifically spelled out in the 'proper prefaces', as we now approach more closely the mystery of our redemption, transacted at the Cross. These proper prefaces for the principal feasts situate the cross within the frame of incarnation and nativity, resurrection, exaltation, bestowal of the Spirit, the coming forth and return of the Father's Son and Spirit, the persons of the Trinity.[24]

Third Cycle: the Communion Proper: the Church as Body of Christ Crucified

After the Sanctus, a third cycle begins: the celebration of Communion itself. This is signalled by the moment of repentance, the Prayer of Humble Access. A concern for the unity of the Eucharistic prayer has resulted in its displacement

---

[24] Thus it is not quite fair to criticize Cranmer for isolating the moment of the Cross: the proper prefaces show that he understands it in relation to these antecedent and consequent moments of redemption – albeit one could ask for more reference to them than just one octave in the year! One of the strongest arguments for the longer Eucharistic prayer of 1549 or the Scottish, American, and Canadian revisions, is that the death of Christ is always related to his resurrection and ascension.

in recent revisions to a later point in the service,[25] but its 1552–1662 location has its own compelling rationale. Just as the prophet Isaiah reacted with penitence to the vision of God adored by angels singing 'Holy, Holy, Holy', so here after the *Sanctus* the congregation responds to the knowledge of God's holiness with repentance and humility.[26] In the presence of supreme holiness, we have learned not to trust in our own righteousness, but in God's manifold and great mercy.

Within this prayer one may detect the triadic movement from repentance to faith to charity at the micro level. The dominant accent, indicated by two clauses, is penitence: 'we do not presume', 'we are not worthy'. But the third sentence moves us towards the second moment of faith: 'But thou art the same Lord, whose property is always to have mercy'. And faith makes us bold to hope for more: 'so to eat the flesh of thy dear Son Jesus Christ, and to drink his blood, that our sinful bodies may be made clean by his body, and our souls washed through his most precious blood, and that we may dwell in him, and he in us'[27] – purification from sin, and mutual indwelling.

---

[25] As a result of the relocation of the Prayer of Humble Access in the American Rite of 1928 and the Canadian Rite of 1962, the moment of Charity in the Sanctus is now followed by the moments of Faith and Charity united in the extended Prayer of Consecration. The moment of Repentance then appears in the Prayer of Humble Access (and *Agnus Dei*) as prelude to the moment of Faith in the Delivery of the Sacrament to the communicants. The elements are all still there, but in a rearrangement which perhaps does not bring out their relation quite as clearly.

[26] Isa. 6. Fr Gary Thorne has brought to my attention the practice of the Eastern liturgies, in which the priest quietly recites Psalm 51 during the singing of the *Sanctus*. One might also compare the penitential *apologiae* which Jungmann (II, 129 n.9) reports to be found at this and other points in many early medieval missals – texts which Cranmer may well have known. The position of the Prayer of Humble Access may thus be not without precedent in the Catholic tradition. See also Calvin, *Institutes* III.iv.11, 'since in every sacred assembly we stand before the sight of God and the angels, what other beginning of our action will there be than the recognition of our own unworthiness?'

[27] The usual mutilation of this prayer in late twentieth-century rites appears to follow a footnote of Dix (*The Shape of the Liturgy*, 1945, pp 611 n1),

The word 'Table' has alerted us to the banquet we approach: the vivid language of eating the body and drinking the blood of Christ indicates that participation in his death makes us partakers of his deathless life. Our hope is in the cross. Sacrifice is what unites us in communion with God – Christ's sacrifice for us, and our sacrifice in him. As Augustine said: 'The true sacrifice is done in every work which is designed to unite us to God in a holy fellowship, every act, that is, which is directed to that final Good which makes possible our true felicity'.[28]

Cranmer's rite is sometimes taken to task – or timidly defended – for its concentration on the motif of sacrifice, and modern Eucharistic rites accordingly boast in the 'richness' of the themes and images they employ. Yet Cranmer's emphasis on sacrifice (for which there is ample precedent in the Roman Canon, the Latin Fathers, and Athanasius) is not arbitrary. One may speak of the atonement as a victory over the powers of evil; but that describes the relation of God and Satan; or as a model of humility, patience, charity, and other virtues: but that describes the relation of Christ to men. It is sacrifice – the offering of the Son to the Father – which concerns the relation of man to God, and accounts for the communion and fellowship of man with *God*. The motifs of victory and moral example find expression elsewhere:[29] it

in which he notes the same theme in Thomas Aquinas, and dismisses it as a 'medieval speculation'. Yet in that passage of the *Summa* (III. Q. 74. Art 1) Thomas was quoting the commentary of a fourth-century exegete (whom Thomas knew as Ambrose but who has been known since Erasmus under the name of Ambrosiaster) on a passage of Leviticus: 'As Ambrose says on 1 Cor. xi.20, this sacrament *avails for the defence of soul and body*; and therefore Christ's body is offered under the species of bread *for the health of the body, and the blood* under the species of wine *for the health of the soul*, according to Leviticus xvii.14: *The life of all flesh is in the blood*'. The 'medieval speculation' turns out to be both patristic and scriptural! Cranmer is here a more authentic transmitter of the faith and worship of the early church than his twentieth-century critics.

[28] Augustine, *The City of God*, x.6.

[29] Thus victory in the Collect for Easter; moral example in the Collect for Palm Sunday.

is sacrifice that matters here, because it is communion with God which is sought.

Accordingly, in the second moment of the cycle, our faith is directed to the mercy of God, active in the willing sacrifice of Christ. This *anamnesis* or memorial of the Father's mercy, the Son's sacrifice, and his institution of the Sacrament, leads into a prayer for real participation in his Body and Blood, by means of the due reception of the sacrament he ordained. The Institution narrative follows, concluding with Christ's own words of command, 'do this'. There is no 'amen':[30] in response to Christ's command the elements are received immediately, with a form of delivery of the elements (the 'words of administration') enjoining their reception with remembrance, faith, and gratitude for his death.[31] Our 'amen' is to receive the elements in the faith which hears, believes, and obeys the words of Christ, 'This is my body ..., This is my Blood ..., Do this, in remembrance of me'.

The note of gratitude sounded in the form of delivery ('and be thankful') leads into the third moment of the cycle, that of the Church's own self-offering in the sacrifice of praise and thanksgiving. This begins, in Cranmer's characteristic way, with the Lord's Prayer, as the first expression of grateful love, of devotion and dependence, of those who are able to approach God as Father through the Son's death (Heb. 10.19). Next follows a choice of prayers, in the complementary language of sacrifice and gratitude. In one prayer we offer 'our sacrifice of praise and thanksgiving', which entails the offering of 'ourselves, our souls and bodies, to be a reasonable, holy, and lively sacrifice'. In the other we acknowledge more fully what benefits we acknowledge in our sacrifice of praise and thanksgiving – God's

---

[30] In 1552 and 1559, though one was (somewhat conventionally) added in 1662.

[31] The 1559 Rite unites the Forms of Delivery found in 1549 and 1552. Though the former ('The Body of Christ ... ', 'The Blood of Christ ...') adapts the traditional language of the sacramental presence, the latter, by exhorting the communicants to gratitude, alludes to the Eucharistic sacrifice.

favour, incorporation into Christ's mystical body, and inheritance of his everlasting kingdom – and also pray for grace to continue in this 'holy fellowship' and in 'good works', which is the content of the self-offering of our lives.

The form of the service both distinguishes the sacrifice of Christ and of his Church – one a sacrifice propitiatory for us, the other a sacrifice Eucharistic in him[32] – and unites them: for it is by the virtue of Christ's sacrifice, as 'very members incorporate of his mystical Body', that we also offer ourselves. The Church is caught up by its appropriation of Christ's sacrifice into his own movement toward the Father.

It is sometimes said that the modern Eucharistic prayers are more fully Trinitarian than Cranmer's narrow focus on Christ and the cross, on account of their rehearsal of the history of salvation in terms of the 'economic' Trinity[33] – the Father's work in creation, the Son's in redemption, the Holy Ghost's in sanctification. Yet if Cranmer's focus is narrow, it is also deeper: he has perceived that in the sacrifice of Christ both for us and in us, is the point where the activity of the economic Trinity, of God's work in creation and salvation, is integrated in the life of the 'immanent' Trinity, the life of God himself. The Eucharistic memorial of Christ's sacrifice is administered precisely so that the faithful communicants may themselves be united in Christ's mystical Body to the return of the Son to the Father in the perfect obedience of his love, and be caught up in the very life of the Trinity.

That is why the relocation of the *Gloria in Excelsis* from its pre-Reformation position (before the Collect) is a masterstroke of liturgical craft. Not only does it now come at the point of greatest joy in the service, but it also serves to express

---

[32] See Cranmer, *Works and Disputations*, (Parker Society, 1844) Vol. 1, p. 346.

[33] The 'economic' Trinity is God in his threefold activity outside himself in creation, redemption and sanctification. It is distinguished from the 'immanent' (or 'theological') Trinity, which refers to the distinction of the three persons within the Godhead.

the heavenly aspect of the Christian community. There is, of course, a long pilgrimage of sanctification yet to be made: we continue praying for grace and mercy in the Prayers after Communion and in the *Gloria in Excelsis*. The relocation of the Gloria shows that the Christian community experiences the graces of justification and sanctification simultaneously; at one and the same time it is both righteous (and thus praising God with the angels in heaven) and sinful (and thus in pilgrimage and prayer for grace still on earth).

The entire motion of the liturgy is one of return to God, through the going forth and return of his Word and Spirit, through the sacrifice of the Incarnate Son, through the Church's preaching of the word and the ministry of the sacrament. Word and Spirit go forth and return, and in their return they bring us with them. Nothing is left behind: earth is caught up into heaven, and man into God; and so the 'heart in pilgrimage' has attained its end. 'Thou hast made us for thyself, O Lord, and our hearts are restless until they find their rest in thee'.[34] Accordingly the congregation is dismissed with an authoritative declaration of God's peace, whereby we are kept 'in the knowledge and love of God'. It is all God, God's knowing and loving the glory of his own infinite goodness through his Word and Spirit, through his Church, so that we may rest in him also, and know that peace which passeth all understanding.

[34] Augustine, *Confessions* 1.1

ANALYSIS OF THE 1559 – 1662 COMMUNION RITE

I   **Preparatory Prayers**
             Lord's Prayer
             'Collect for Purity'

II   **The General Preparation for Communion**

Repentance	Decalogue and Responses
	Collect for King
	Collect of Day
Faith	Epistle lesson
	Gospel lesson
	Creed
	Sermon
	Notices of holy days, fasting days, banns, etc.
Charity	Sentences & collection of alms and offerings
	Prayer for 'the whole state of Christ's Church militant here on earth'

III   **Immediate Preparation for Communion**

Repentance	Three Exhortations
	Invitation
	Confession of Sin
Faith	Absolution
	Comfortable Words
Charity	Sursum Corda, Preface,
	Sanctus

IV   **Celebration of Communion**

Repentance	'Prayer of Humble Access'
Faith	'Prayer of Consecration'
	Delivery of sacrament (Communion proper)
Charity	Lord's Prayer
	One of two post-Communion Prayers (Thanksgiving and Self-Oblation)
	Gloria in Excelsis

V   **Dismissal of Congregation**
The declaration of the Peace and the Blessing of God

The Bible in the Prayer Book: The Place, the Text, the Teaching and the Interpretation of the Bible in the Book of Common Prayer

Roger Beckwith

The Revd Dr Roger Beckwith grew up on the border between the St Albans and London dioceses, and first encountered the Church of England in the parish of Monken Hadley, where the Book of Common Prayer was the liturgy in use. He has since continued to love and admire it, has taught liturgy at theological Colleges, and has written a good deal on this and other theological subjects. He studied at Oxford and Bristol, and was awarded a Lambeth D.D. by the former Archbishop of Canterbury, George Carey.

One needs only to read the homily which Thomas Cranmer placed at the head of the first *Book of Homilies*, 'A fruitful Exhortation to the Reading and Knowledge of Holy Scripture', or the preface he wrote for the second edition of Tyndale and Coverdale's *Great Bible*, to realise how concerned he was to promote the reading and hearing of the words of Scripture. But this concern is expressed more succinctly, and even more memorably, in the Prayer Book Collect that he composed for the Second Sunday in Advent:

Blessed Lord, who hast caused all holy Scriptures to be written for our learning: Grant that we may in such wise hear them, read, mark, learn, and inwardly digest them, that by patience and comfort of thy holy Word, we may embrace and ever hold fast the blessed hope of everlasting life, which thou hast given us in our Saviour Jesus Christ. Amen.

Cranmer evidently realised that to *hear* the Scriptures was a different experience from *reading* them, and could only happen in public or at least in company. It could not be hurried, and was beneficial to those who had not learnt to read them for themselves as well as to those who had. Those who had learnt to read could also read in private, but with half the population at that period illiterate, he was especially concerned for the reading and hearing of the Scriptures in public, where the whole nation could take part. So, as he explains in his Preface to the Prayer Book, now called 'Concerning the Service of the Church', he had drawn up a new daily lectionary for use at Morning and Evening Prayer, in which more or less the whole of the Bible and some of the Apocrypha was read in the course of a year, in an orderly manner and in English. (Among the exceptions, none of the Song of Solomon was read and only two chapters of Revelation, for fear of misunderstanding, though four more chapters of Revelation were read as Epistles at Holy Communion). No special provision was made for Sundays in the daily lectionary, but only for Holy Days, as it was evidently hoped that the laity, no less than the clergy, would be able to be present on weekdays as well as Sundays to hear the Bible read in continuous sequence. It was a noble vision, but destined to be frustrated by the realities of everyday life. For as early as 1561, in the opening years of Elizabeth's reign, it was found necessary to prepare a special table of lessons for Sundays, for the benefit of those who could get to church on no other day, and this provision, with some development, has been continued ever since.

The Psalter, as had been customary since Jewish times, was given special treatment, and in the Prayer Book it was divided into 30 morning and 30 evening portions, to be read at the daily services each month. One slightly surprising feature is that Psalm 134 occurs among the morning psalms, though it is addressed to those who stand in the house of the Lord by night. Perhaps this can be understood as referring to the morning watch, the last portion of the night, when the day is just beginning (Exod. 14.24). The Psalms (now with the numbering of the Hebrew Bible, not of the Greek and Latin) were printed in the Prayer Book according to Coverdale's translation in the Great Bible, which was the Bible translation customarily used in Cranmer's time. They became so popular that they were left in the same translation at the 1662 revision, when the Authorized Version of 1611 was substituted in the case of the Epistles and Gospels (see the 1662 Preface).

Four of the Psalms were used also as Canticles at Morning and Evening Prayer, and in 1662, these likewise were left in Coverdale's translation (apart from the extra 'Yea' in the fifth verse of the Deus Misereatur, which is not in Coverdale or in the Authorised Version). The other four Canticles from the Bible or the Apocrypha (the Benedicite, the Benedictus, the Magnificat and the Nunc Dimittis), being popular like the Psalms, were kept by the 1662 revisers in the translation of the Great Bible.

Apart from the readings at Morning and Evening Prayer, the Prayer Book also of course contains another great series of Scripture readings, the Epistles and Gospels for Holy Communion. These, like the Psalter, are printed in the Prayer Book, and, as we have already noted, they follow the text of the Authorized Version. Being printed in the Prayer Book allows them to be grouped with their respective Collects, and, since they are appointed only for Sundays and Holy Days, they do not absorb the inordinate amount of space which the daily readings would. The choice of readings for the Epistles and Gospels, generally but not invariably, follows the choice reflected in the pre-Reformation liturgy. An Old Testament passage is occasionally appointed to be used instead of an Epistle, but the main provision for the reading of the Old Testament is at Morning and Evening Prayer.

The Prayer Book contains various collections of texts on particular subjects, from which, if not read in full, suitable selections can be made by the minister conducting the service. There are the penitential sentences at the beginning of Morning and Evening Prayer; there are the offertory sentences and the Comfortable Words in the Holy Communion service; there are the sentences on marriage at the end of the Marriage service; and there are the introductory sentences to the Burial service. All these were adapted at the 1662 revision to conform to the Authorized Version, except the ones in the service of Holy Communion, which were kept unchanged.

The basic difference between the Authorized Version and the Great Bible is an improvement in accuracy. Both aimed to be translations of the original Hebrew and Greek, not of the Latin Vulgate, as Wycliffe's translation had been, but this was more fully achieved in Tyndale's portion of the Great Bible, since Coverdale was dependent on recent intermediate translations into German and Latin, whereas Tyndale was learned in the original languages. Tyndale was responsible for the New Testament and a considerable part of the Old, whereas Coverdale was responsible for the remaining books. In the Authorized Version, unlike the Great Bible, the whole of both Testaments was translated directly from the Hebrew and Greek.

The Lord's Prayer and the Ten Commandments

There are two biblical texts of particular importance, which appear a number of times in the Prayer Book, and which candidates for confirmation are expected to learn by heart. These are the Lord's Prayer and the Ten Commandments. The Lord's Prayer occurs twice in each of the daily services and the Holy Communion service and once in the Catechism, apart from other occurrences. The Ten Commandments occur once in the Holy Communion service and once in the Catechism.

The Lord's Prayer always appears in the same form, from the first (1549) edition of the Prayer Book onwards, except that in 1662, for the first time, it sometimes appears with the doxology added. This happens once in Morning and Evening Prayer and once in Holy Communion, but on the other occasion in each of the three services it appears without the doxology, as it also does in the Catechism and in most other services. The addition of the doxology seems to be due to the fact that in 1611 the translators of the Authorized Version had decided that the doxology should occur in St Matthew's text of the Lord's Prayer, though it did not in St Luke's, and though it had previously not appeared in the Prayer Book at all. Otherwise, the Prayer Book text of the Lord's Prayer is always the same, though it comes from no known translation of the Bible, and seems to have been slightly adapted by Cranmer (who was familiar with biblical languages) from Tyndale's wording.

Much the same appears to be the case with the Ten Commandments. They first appear in the Prayer Book in the Catechism. This is in 1549, where the longer Commandments are abbreviated. In 1552, however, they are printed in full, and the same text of them is introduced into the Holy Communion service, with only the reference to deliverance from Egypt being omitted. Then in 1662 the same text is used again in both places. It is neither the text of the Great Bible nor the text of the Authorized Version, and appears to be another slight adaptation by Cranmer, designed to make the wording as readable and as memorable as possible.

The Ascension Day Gospel
The Gospel for Ascension Day is taken from the latter part of Mark 16, as was already the custom before the Reformation. Up to the nineteenth century this would have presented no problem, but textual criticism has since taught modern man to regard what is now called the Longer Ending of Mark with suspicion. It does not occur in the two great fourth-century manuscripts of the Greek Bible, Codex Vaticanus and Codex

Sinaiticus, in which Mark's Gospel ends very abruptly at verse 8 of the last chapter, without the account of the resurrection appearances of Jesus or of his ascension into heaven. This may indeed mean that the original ending of the Gospel had got detached and lost at a very early period, and that the two codices were copied from manuscripts in which it did not occur, but as early as the second century copies with the Longer Ending were in circulation, and were accepted as authentic by learned writers such as Irenaeus. So there is nothing to prevent us believing that, quite shortly after the original ending was lost, God moved someone to add a suitable replacement, which is what we now have.

Of course, it is not only in quoted passages that the Bible appears in the Prayer Book. Such was Cranmer's love and reverence for the Bible that its teaching and language appear everywhere in his liturgy. In the old book by H. I. Bailey (1845), *The Liturgy compared with the Bible*, London: SPCK, portions of which have more recently been reprinted by the Harrison Trust,[1] the whole spoken text of the Prayer Book is reproduced, accompanied throughout by the supporting passages of Scripture on which each part is based.

The Teaching of the Bible as reflected in the Prayer Book

If it be asked what, in brief, is biblical teaching, as we find it in the Prayer Book, the answer is ready to hand. The Prayer Book Catechism, which is really the basic manual of teaching for all Anglican Christians, despite contemporary neglect, sets important biblical passages before us as our model of conduct (the Ten Commandments, from Exodus 20) and as our model of prayer (the Lord's Prayer, from Matthew 6 and Luke 11). Since the Bible does not contain a similar brief model of *belief*, the Catechism uses one based on the Bible and drawn up by the early church, the Apostles' Creed, which it summarizes as teaching us 'to believe in God the Father, who hath made me,

---

[1] H. I. Bailey (1999), *Morning and Evening Prayer and the Bible* and *The Lord's Supper or Holy Communion and the Bible*, The Harrison Trust.

and all the world'; 'in God the Son, who hath redeemed me, and all mankind'; and 'in God the Holy Ghost, who sanctifieth me, and all the elect people of God'. Thus it is God who confers each of these benefits, but as there are three Persons in the one God, we are taught to believe that the Father is particularly responsible for our creation, the Son for our redemption and the Holy Spirit for our sanctification. The teaching on creation is derived especially from the Old Testament (Gen. 1–2, as interpreted in the New Testament), and the teaching on redemption and sanctification especially from the New Testament (the Gospels, Acts and Epistles). The Prayer Book appoints the Apostles' Creed and two other ancient creeds, the Nicene Creed (in the Holy Communion service) and the Athanasian Creed (under the heading 'At Morning Prayer'), to be used in its services, and thus indicates the intention of the Church of England to teach the faith of the historic, orthodox church of the realm, which is also the faith taught in the Bible, without altering it or (still less) substituting anything else.

The Catechism similarly summarizes the Ten Commandments and the Lord's Prayer, in the former case relating them to the two great Commandments in the Law singled out by our Lord, the love of God and of our neighbour (Deut. 6.4–5; Lev. 19.18), so that the first four of the Ten Commandments are expressions of the love of God, and the last six expressions of the love of our neighbour.

The Catechism ends with teaching on the two sacraments of Baptism and the Lord's Supper, which were subjects of controversy at the time when it was drawn up (the latter especially) and have remained such since. Both sacraments were ordained by Christ himself in the Gospels, and his teaching about them is basic, though it is expanded in the Epistles. Both sacraments are means of spiritual grace, and both should be received with repentance and faith, though when infants are baptized, sureties speak on their behalf until they reach the years of discretion. The saving grace received in baptism is a death unto sin and a new birth unto righteousness, and that received in the Lord's Supper is the feeding of our souls on the body and blood of Christ, as we thankfully commemorate his atoning death. Further teaching on baptism is found in the opening words of the Catechism, and the teaching on both sacraments is also reflected in the services for the administration of them both.

Formal teaching on the Last Things is explicit only in the concluding part of each of the three Creeds.

The teaching of the Creeds and Catechism on many subjects is amplified by the Thirty-nine Articles and the *Book of Homilies* (see Articles 11 and 35), in both of which works Cranmer had a large share, and both of which have lawful authority, direct or indirect. The *Book of Homilies*, after being out of print for most of the twentieth century, has since 2006 been available in a handsome new edition.[2]

Some Particular Points of Interpretation
So much for the place that the Bible has in the Prayer Book, the text of it that we find there, and its teaching. In conclusion, we will look at a few interesting examples of biblical interpretation that are reflected in the Prayer Book.

Festivals of Apostles
The Prayer Book provides festivals for each of our Lord's 12 apostles, including Matthias the substitute for Judas Iscariot, and it groups four of them in two pairs, Philip with James the son of Alphaeus, and Simon the Zealot with Judas *not* Iscariot. This follows pre-Reformation custom. However, it provides new Epistles for these last two festivals, from the Epistle of James and from the Epistle of Jude (in Greek Judas). In the New Testament, the name James, without further identification, means James the Lord's brother, and Jude in his Epistle calls himself the brother of James. We know that two of the Lord's four brothers were named James and Judas (Mt. 13.55; Mk 6.3). So the question arises, is the Prayer Book implying,

---

[2] *The Homilies*, ed. John Griffiths, revised Ian Robinson (2006), Brynmill and Preservation Press.

by its choice of Epistles, that these brothers of the Lord were identical with two of the apostles? Not necessarily, since Jn 7.5 tells us that during Jesus' ministry his brothers did not believe in him: they only did so after his death and resurrection (Acts 1.14), perhaps following his resurrection appearance to James (1 Cor. 15.7). More probably, the Prayer Book is linking them with their apostolic namesakes because of the importance of the Lord's brothers in the apostolic church (1 Cor. 9.5). What is meant by calling them Jesus' brothers has been much discussed, but the most ancient opinion seems to be that they were not younger brothers but older brothers, born to Joseph by a previous wife.

St Barnabas the Apostle

The only other saint to whom the Prayer Book gives the title of 'apostle', apart from the Twelve and St Paul, is Barnabas. This follows pre-Reformation custom, and has the authority of Acts 14.14, where we read of 'the apostles Barnabas and Paul'. This wording may mean apostles of the Church of Antioch, by whom they were sent out in verses 3–4 of the previous chapter (compare 2 Cor. 8.23, where the 'messengers of the churches' are in Greek *apostoloi*), but since they were sent out at the command of God (Acts 13.2), the Collect is entitled to call Barnabas '*thy* holy apostle Barnabas', as it does.

St Luke the Evangelist

The Prayer Book calls St Luke 'the Evangelist' primarily, no doubt, as being the author of the third Gospel (and of its sequel the Acts of the Apostles). He can also be called an evangelist, however, as a preacher of the Gospel and a companion of St Paul in his evangelistic journeys. He began to fulfil this role as early as St Paul's second missionary journey of about AD 49–50, when he first begins to use the famous 'we' language in his account of the journey in Acts 16.10–17. The phrase in the Collect for his festival 'whose praise is in the gospel' is derived from 2 Cor. 8.18, where 'the brother whose praise is in the gospel throughout all the churches' is traditionally believed to be Luke. 2 Corinthians was written about AD 56, so the phrase could well refer to Luke's ministry as Paul's companion, which he already was, though his ministry as the author of the Gospel would be mostly still in the future. The Collect also calls him 'Luke the Physician', which is derived from the touching words of Col. 4.14, 'Luke the beloved physician'.

St Stephen the First Martyr

St Stephen is celebrated at two places in the Prayer Book. The first is at the provisions for his festival on 26 December, with a Collect, Epistle and Gospel, and with special readings in the daily table of lessons. His Collect draws attention to his sufferings, his witness, his faith, his forgiveness of his murderers, and the way Jesus helped him in his hour of need. The second place is in the Ordering of Deacons, where Acts 6 is set as an alternative Epistle, and the Collect reflects the traditional view of the meaning of this passage, namely, that Stephen and his six companions were being appointed to the order of deacons. The fact that the passage does not explicitly say so, and that elsewhere in the Acts of the Apostles the duty of serving tables in the Jerusalem church seems to be assigned not to deacons but to presbyters (Acts 11.30), has recently caused some to doubt this interpretation. What is certainly true, however, is that Stephen and his companions in Acts 6 were being appointed to an assistant role, so that they could help the apostles in their work, in much the way that deacons help presbyters in their work today.

For Further Reading

H. I. Bailey, *The Liturgy compared with the Bible* (see reference above).

F. E. Brightman (1970), *The English Rite* (reprinted), Gregg, which gives the various editions of the English Prayer Book and its sources in parallel columns.

F. F. Bruce (1961), *The English Bible*, London: Lutterworth,

which is an illuminating account of the various English
translations of the Bible up to the mid-twentieth century.
W. K. Clay, *Liturgical Services of the Reign of Queen Elizabeth*,
    Parker Society, which on page 437 gives the 1561 lectionary
    for Sundays.

The Lectionaries in the Book of Common Prayer

David Phillips

The Revd David Phillips is a Canadian serving in the Diocese of Gibraltar in Europe as Chaplain at Holy Cross in Palermo, Sicily. He became an Anglican soon after hearing his first Book of Common Prayer service at All Saints' Rome in his twenties. He studied Divinity at Wycliffe College in Toronto and has served in Canada as a parish priest in two Prayer Book parishes and as executive archdeacon in Saskatchewan. He is webmaster of Lectionary Central and is currently writing a book on the spiritual ascent based on the Prayer Book lectionary.

To a Christian man there can be nothing either more necessary or profitable, than the knowledge of holy Scripture, forasmuch as in it is contained God's true word, setting forth his glory, and also man's duty ... And there is no truth nor doctrine necessary for our justification and everlasting salvation, but that is (or may be) drawn out of that fountain and Well of truth.

> From the Homily 'A Fruitful Exhortation to the reading of Holy Scripture'.

Here may all manner of persons, men, women, young, old, learned, unlearned, rich, poor, priests, laymen, lords, ladies, officers, tenants, and mean men, virgins, wives, widows, lawyers, merchants, artificers, husbandmen, and all manner of persons of what estate or condition soever they be, may in this book learn all things what they ought to believe, what they ought to do, and what they should not do, as well concerning almighty God, as also concerning themselves and all other.

Cranmer, from the Preface to the Great Bible.

If you read the Preface to the first Book of Common Prayer (1549) you will see very quickly that the ordered reading of Scripture (the lectionaries) is of foremost importance to the whole project of Common Prayer in the English Reformation.[1] In the first two paragraphs of the Preface we read *solely* about how Scripture has been and should be read. The English Reformers, like their Continental counterparts, had taken up the call to return to Scripture as the sole basis for determining Christian doctrine and that the Bible should be placed freely in the hands of all people so that its saving doctrine might be 'drawn out of that fountain and Well of truth'.

The Bible is to be read by all – but how should it be read in and by the Church?

The Preface to the Prayer Book states, regarding the 'ordering of the divine service', that in ancient times the whole of Scripture was read each year by the clergy and heard also in the church by the laity. Next the Preface refers to the corruption of the divine service with the addition of 'uncertain Stories and Legends' and that these have been removed so that 'nothing is ordained to be read, but the very pure Word of God, the holy Scriptures, or that which is agreeable to the same'. The inclusion of the whole Psalter is meant to recover the reading of all the psalms regularly, not just a few of the same psalms repeated each day. In the Preface we learn that the overall plan for the selection of readings was to be simplified so that no longer would it be 'more business to find out what should be

---

[1] The Preface to the 1549 Book of Common Prayer is the second part of the Preface to the 1662 Book of Common Prayer.

read, than to read it when it was found out'. It is simplified, not only for clergy, but with the idea that daily prayer, including the reading of Scripture, is the task of all Christians 'of what estate or condition soever they be'. Scripture is to be read 'in a Language and Order as is most easy and plain for the understanding both of the Readers and Hearers'.

The Book of Common Prayer contains within it a combination of lectionaries for the ordered reading of Scripture:[2]

1 **Eucharistic Lectionary**: This is the series of Epistle and Gospel readings for use at Holy Communion services on Sundays and holy days. The Reformation standardized across England the use of the ancient lectionary from the Sarum Missal (the service book used in Salisbury Cathedral). These readings are printed in full and so constitute a major portion, about 30 per cent of the overall content of the Book of Common Prayer. The inclusion of this lectionary with very minor changes (described below) imports into the heart of the common prayer tradition the teaching of the early Church and a particular way of reading the Scriptures. The origins and development of this lectionary and its logic is looked at in detail below.

2 **Daily Office Lectionary**: To this core Eucharistic Lectionary is added Old and New Testament lessons for each day of the year to be read at the daily offices of Morning and Evening Prayer. The appointed readings are found in an easily understood table at the beginning of the Prayer Book.

The Daily Office lectionary has gone through revisions over the centuries. In 1871 a revision was made so that the

[2] See Curry, D. P., 'Doctrinal Instrument of Salvation: The Use of Scripture in the Prayer Book Lectionary', in *The Prayer Book: A Theological Conference held at St. Peter's Cathedral, Charlottetown, P.E.I. June 25th–28th, 1985*, for a comprehensive account of the use of Scripture in the Prayer Book, the historical background of the Eucharistic and daily office lectionaries and a comparison with and critique of modern lectionaries. This paper can be read online at: www.lectionarycentral.com/Curry1.html

New Testament was read twice instead of three times[3] in the year, once at Morning Prayer and once at Evening Prayer. This meant shorter readings and also that a lay person who could only attend the Morning or the Evening service would hear the whole of the New Testament each year. Portions of Revelation were appointed for Advent. This is the 'Calendar, with Table of Lessons' found at the beginning of current editions of the 1662 Book of Common Prayer.

A 1922 revision and a proposed revision in 1955 has meant that there is now more than one Daily Office lectionary possible following the Prayer Book tradition.[4] In these revisions, close to the same amount of Scripture is read as in 1871, but in an order following the Church year rather than the calendar year. Books of the Bible follow a course of consecutive reading, but the books are read in the most appropriate time in the Church year. For example, as Isaiah had been read in Advent in the original lectionary, now Genesis is read beginning in Septuagesima and follows through Exodus in Lent. The lessons on our Creation, Fall, the early covenants and Exodus remind us of the preparation in history for the redemption wrought by our Lord on the Cross. These modern revisions to the Daily Office lectionary in the Prayer Book make it much closer to that used in the early Church and greatly inform and enrich the understanding and teaching of the Sunday Eucharistic lectionary.

---

[3] In the first Prayer Book and up until 1871, the whole or the greater part of the Old Testament and Apocrypha was read once a year beginning in January. The Old Testament readings began with Genesis (Morning and Evening), and followed a course of consecutive readings, except that Isaiah was reserved for Advent. The New Testament was read three times, the Gospels at Morning Prayer, Acts and the Epistles at Evening Prayer, but Revelation was omitted. The consecutive readings were interrupted only on unmoveable feast days.

[4] The 1922 revision was authorized and is printed as an alternative in some editions of the 1662 BCP. The 1955 revision was never authorized but was widely used at the time and was later incorporated in the 1962 Canadian revision of the BCP.

3 **Sunday Office Lectionary:** The Book of Common Prayer also includes a table of readings for use at the Sunday and Holy Day Offices of Morning and Evening Prayer. In the first Prayer Book, provision was only made for an Old Testament lesson that related generally to the season. In revisions in the Church of England since, there has been a gradual move to fill out Old and New Testament readings and, as in the Daily Office Lectionary, to relate them to the Sunday Eucharistic lectionary following the Church year.

4 **The Psalter:** All of the Psalms are printed in full in the Book of Common Prayer and they are divided into 60 parts to be read through each month at the Daily Offices (a 30-day cycle, morning and evening). On months with 31 days, the psalms appointed for day 30 are to be repeated on day 31. The Psalter is also at the heart of the English common prayer tradition and like the Eucharistic lectionary constitutes about 30 per cent of the content of the Book of Common Prayer. It is the book of the Bible in the Prayer Book lectionaries that is appointed to be read the most – over 12 times per year. Because the whole Psalter is appointed for use in worship, and so regularly, we are taught how to pray through all of the vicissitudes of life using the very words of Scripture. As Jesus and the Apostles refer to the Psalms more than any other book of the Bible, and see them speaking prophetically of Christ and the Church, so do we learn a devotional and spiritual mode of reading Scripture, as in the early Church.[5]

[5] See Blunt, J. H. (1872), *The Annotated Book of Common Prayer: Being an Historical, Ritual and Theological Commentary on the Devotional System of the Church of England*, London, Oxford and Cambridge: Rivingtons, Sixth Edition, p. 316: 'This spiritual mode of viewing the Psalms was the principal if not the only one adopted by the early Church. 'All the Psalms', says St. Jerome, 'appertain to the Person of Christ'. 'David more than all the rest of the prophets,' says St. Ambrose, 'spake of the marriage between the Divine and Human nature'. Tertullian had declared that nearly all the Psalms represent the Son speaking to the Father; and St Hilary leaves his opinion on record, that all which is in the Psalms refers to the knowledge of the coming of our Lord Jesus Christ, His Incarnation, Passion, and Resurrection, and to

The whole pattern of ordered reading of Scripture, the lectionaries, is either printed in full or explained in easily understood
tables at the beginning of each Book of Common Prayer. The
Reformers met their goal that no longer would it be 'more
business to find out what should be read, than to read it when
it was found out'.

Today, there is little appreciation in the Anglican Communion
of the importance or spiritual depth of the Sunday Eucharistic
lectionary in the Book of Common Prayer. Few Anglican
clerics today use this as the primary lectionary on Sundays and
as a basis for preaching and teaching and many assume there
is little logic to its selection of readings, especially in Trinity
season. What follows in the rest of this chapter is an attempt
to make known something of its importance and riches and to
revive an interest in its use.

Some Preliminaries about the Sunday Eucharistic Lectionary
Origins and History
For about 1000 years before the Reformation, the Church in
the West had a selection of readings to be used on Sundays
at the Eucharist and on occasional holy days throughout
the year. This traditional Western Eucharistic lectionary is
from the *Comes of St. Jerome*, a lectionary attributed to St
Jerome. While its precise origin is unknown, there is evidence
that it may be as ancient as the fifth century, the time of the
Latin Church Fathers. Variations in the Eucharistic lectionaries in Europe occurred in the Middle Ages. For example,
in the lectionary found in the Roman Missal, the addition
of a Gospel reading early in Trinity season sometime in the
Middle Ages meant a dislocation of the Epistles from the
corresponding Gospels in the Sunday Eucharistic lectionary

the glory also and power of our own life in Him. Such habits of thought were
partly inherited from the Jews, who could see the Messiah in their ancient
prophesies ... But without going back to the Jews, we may trace this clear
vision of Christ in the Psalms to the Apostles themselves, and from them to
the teaching of His own lips and example.'

for the rest of the Church year. However, in the Sarum Missal, the same dislocation had not happened. When the Reformers chose the Sarum lectionary, they preserved the lectionary from the *Comes of St. Jerome*. This ancient lectionary remains remarkably intact in the Anglican Communion, as in no other Church, in the 1662 Book of Common Prayer to this day.

The Anglican Reformers in the sixteenth century chose to have the Church of England continue with this same selection of Epistle and Gospel readings for Sundays and Holy days with a few minor changes over the year: sixteen of the readings were lengthened by a few verses, seven were shortened by a few verses, and ten lessons (either a Lesson, Epistle or Gospel, primarily in the Christmas and Easter seasons) were changed.[6] These minor changes show both that the Reformers considered the lectionary carefully and, in retaining the ancient lectionary, they indicated their satisfaction with the Scripture choices, with the way of reading Scripture that this choice implied, and with the use of the Church year as a logically ordered helpful way of proclaiming and teaching the faith.

In the 1662 revision of the Book of Common Prayer, the Eucharistic lectionary remained unchanged except for the addition of readings for the Sixth Sunday after Epiphany and the shortening of Gospel readings during Holy Week. The choice of lections was not changed but the English translation used in the Prayer Book was revised to include the Authorized or King James Version, rather than the translation from the Great Bible of 1540.

The Collects
The Collects in the Book of Common Prayer are the prayers appointed for use each Sunday and for the week. They have always been seen as a treasure to the Church – so much so, that even in modern liturgies, many have been retained. But

---

[6] The lections that were changed were as follows (G=Gospel; E=Epistle): Christmas 1 G; Christmas 2 E+G; Epiphany E (E replaced an OT lesson); Epiphany 4 E; Easter Eve E+G; Easter Day E+G; Trinity 15 E.

strangely, alongside the newer lectionaries, they normally no longer 'collect' the thought of the readings.

But when the Collects are read in their original context, with the Prayer Book Eucharistic lectionary, they, with a few exceptions, become the very key to help unlock the main idea linking the Epistle and Gospel readings. The exceptions are the Collects in the latter part of Trinity season (Trinity 17–24) that were for some reason, during the Middle Ages, displaced from the lections they had originally been appointed with.

At the Reformation, the Collects were translated from Latin to English, sometimes reflecting a Reformation emphasis. In a few cases, in the first half of the Church year, new Collects were written, based upon and using the very words from the lections of the day. In these new compositions it is clear that the Reformers saw the Collects as being the key to 'collect' the main idea of the lections.

A Way of Reading Scripture

The decision by the Reformers to maintain the same lectionary choices is important in retaining key passages to teach the faith, but also because in their location in the Church year and their combination of Epistle and Gospel together, they embody a certain way of reading and interpreting Scripture. For example, in looking for the connections between the Epistle and Gospel for any Sunday, one learns to understand the miracles of Jesus in a symbolical way, and at times the actions of our Lord in the Gospels are read as a parable of the spiritual life. The best recent writer on this subject is a Canadian Anglican patristics scholar, the late Revd Dr Robert Crouse. The way of reading Scripture and the logic behind the readings for the first half of the church year have been explicated well by Crouse in his sermons.

Consider, for example, the first Sunday in Advent. The ancient Gospel is the account of the coming of Jesus to Jerusalem and the adoration by the crowds with palms (Mt. 21.1–11). The only change the Reformers made was to include the account of the cleansing of the Temple which follows immediately (vv. 12–13). At first it may seem strange to have the Palm Sunday Gospel read here. But the Gospel is to be read as a parable of Advent as we think upon Christ's original visit in the flesh, and his coming again one day at the end of time and the judgement that his presence brought then and will bring.[7] But the Temple of the Old Testament is understood in the New Testament as an image of the body or the soul.[8] The Epistle is all about the soul being awakened and cleansed of works of darkness and filled with light as we 'put on Christ'.[9] It is about Christ's present coming to our soul, God's temple, which brings judgement and cleansing now and prepares us for the final judgement when he returns. The Gospel is to be read in a spiritual way as a parable of Christ's coming to our soul in the present.

To understand the way in which the miracles of Jesus are symbolical, consider the Gospel reading for Quinquagesima Sunday, the Sunday before Lent. The Gospel begins with the blindness of the disciples to the meaning of the coming passion and death of Christ. When Jesus told them about it, we learn that the disciples 'understood none of these things: and this saying was hid from them, neither knew they the things which were spoken'. Immediately after this they meet a blind man, sitting by the wayside, who begs Jesus to give him his sight. A spiritual reading of this Gospel links the two circumstances together as providential. The Church placed this Gospel in the context of the last Sunday before Lent, because we are to link it with our own circumstance: we are blind to the full implications of the Cross, and so we must go up to Jerusalem with Jesus once again through Lent that our blindness, through

---

[7] See Crouse's sermon at: www.lectionarycentral.com/advent1/Crouse2.html
[8] See for example Jesus in Jn 2.19 and St Paul in 1 Cor. 3.16, 17; 1 Cor. 6.16; 2 Cor. 6.16. The idea of God drawing near in the Old Covenant and being manifested in a special way in the midst of Israel in the Tabernacle is a clear forerunner to God's greater promise in the New Covenant, made possible by Christ's death, to dwell in the very hearts of believers (Jn 14.15–23).
[9] The original Epistle Rom. 13.11–14, was lengthened by the Reformers by adding vs. 8–10, but the core idea is in the original Epistle.

faith, will be turned into sight. This combination of a teaching followed by a miracle in the Gospel directs us to see the miracle as symbolical (see also the Gospel for Trinity 17)[10]. In the Eucharistic lectionary, when there is a Gospel miracle without a parallel teaching within the Gospel, the Epistle often brings out the symbolical meaning.

Trying to understand the logic for the choices of Epistle and Gospel together opens one to a way of reading Scriptures through the eyes of the Early Church theologians rooted in but going beyond the literal in all its richness and psychological depth.

The Logic of the Sunday Eucharistic Lectionary

In the centuries since the Reformation, commentators on the Book of Common Prayer have summarized their understanding of the reason behind the choice of readings during the Church year. There is widespread agreement in Prayer Book commentaries that the Church year can be divided into two main parts. The first half, from Advent to Whit Sunday, takes us through the various elements of our Creed, teaching us the faith. The second half of the Church year, Trinity season, begins with Trinity Sunday and ends with the Sunday Next before Advent. Anglican Church divines and Prayer Book commentaries are in agreement that Trinity season is about our sanctification, our growth in holiness in Christ, the practical duties of living the virtuous Christian life.

Why did the Reformers continue with this lectionary largely unchanged?

The Reformation Church in England, as evidenced in her Liturgy, her Articles, her Homilies, desired precisely to show

---

[10] This is not to suggest that the miracles did not literally happen or that they were not performed by Christ to reveal his divinity and so strengthen faith, but to say that the purpose of the miracles is also to teach eternal spiritual truths in a symbolical way. John Calvin, the greatest Reformation exegete, agreed with this early Church understanding of the purpose of the miracles (see for example his commentary on Lk. 8:39 and the editor's note).

that they were not teaching a new faith, but the faith of the Early Church, purified and cleansed of confusions of the later medieval period. As the first half of the Church year contains key Scripture passages to teach us the faith outlined in our Creeds defined by the fifth century, prior to the lectionary, there was no need to change them. The doctrines of the Creed are fully taught as we follow through in the first half of the Church year the birth, life, passion and death, resurrection and ascension of Christ and the sending forth of the Holy Spirit at Pentecost. The new Reformation emphasis on justification, meant not teaching a *new* faith but the same faith by which we are *justified*. The Reformers also saw no need to change the teaching revealed in Scripture about holiness of life and the call to good works, as found in the lections in Trinity season.

What follows is a suggestion of the logic in the seasons through the Church year in these two major parts.

From Advent to Whit Sunday – The Faith by which We are Justified

The lections chosen for the feast days and seasons of Christmas, Easter, Ascension and Pentecost unfold in a clear way the doctrines of the Incarnation, Resurrection, Ascension and the sending of the Holy Ghost. What follows is a brief description of the way the readings have been set out in the seasons of Advent, Epiphany, Pre-Lent and Lent.

Advent

Crouse notes that 'St. Thomas Aquinas, in the Prologue of his commentary on Isaiah, speaks of [the] three dimensions of Advent: the coming of the Son of God *in carne*: in the flesh, historically; his coming *in mente*: in our souls, now by grace; and *ad judicium*: at the judgement, at the end and as the end of history. Paramount in our Advent lessons is that second dimension: Christ's Advent *in mente*, the present coming of the Word of God in our souls by grace. If you were to look at the lessons from that standpoint, you would notice how in each case the Epistle lesson underlines the present reference of the

Gospel lesson'.[11] This has been demonstrated in the example
given above on Advent I in the section *A Way of Reading
Scripture.*

These three dimensions of Advent – Christ's past, future
coming, and most importantly his present coming – are
reflected beautifully in the Collect for the First Sunday in
Advent, which is to be repeated throughout the season:

> Almighty God, give us grace that we may cast away the
> works of darkness, and put upon us the armour of light,
> *now* in the time of this mortal life, in which thy Son Jesus
> Christ *came* to visit us in great humility; that in the last
> day, when he shall *come again* in his glorious Majesty, to
> judge both the quick and the dead, we may rise to the life
> immortal ...

Epiphany
Epiphany season is a drawing out of the meaning and implications of Christmas, of the Incarnation. We follow the
revelations of God in the flesh as we follow Jesus' earthly life
in the Gospels: first as an infant king born for Jew and Gentile
alike; then Jesus as a teenager revealed as the Wisdom of God
disputing with the teachers in the Temple; next, in Jesus' first
miracle at Canaan turning water into wine and so revealing
the arrival of the promised Messianic Age; then as the Power
of God come to restore humanity and human community
revealed by his miracles.

In each Sunday the corresponding Epistles show the
related 'epiphany' of Christ in the present to and in the soul
of the believer. For example, the Epistle appointed with the
Gospel of Christ as a teenager disputing with the doctors

[11] Crouse, R. D., *Advent Meditations*, originally presented by Dr Crouse
for the Prayer Book Society of Canada, Nova Scotia/Prince Edward Island
Branch Advent 2002 Institute, held at St George's Round Church, Halifax,
30 November 2002. This paper is available on Lectionary Central at: www.
lectionarycentral.com/advent1/Crouse1to4.html.

in the Temple contains the injunction to 'be transformed by the renewing of your mind' (and includes the relation of that renewal of the mind to holiness and humility). The Epistle appointed with the Gospel of the miracle at the wedding of Canaan, is about how the Spirit transforms our natural gifts into what is supernatural. The healing of a Jew and a Gentile in the Gospel for Epiphany III is accompanied by a call in the Epistle to show mercy and to live peaceably with all people whether friend or enemy, as Jesus shows us in the Gospel.[12]

Pre-Lent and Lent
Pre-Lent, the three Sundays before Lent, call us to pilgrimage with Jesus during the season of Lent – that we might 'go up to Jerusalem' with Jesus. The names of these ancient Sundays – Septuagesima, Sexagesima and Quinquagesima – refer to the approximate number of days to Easter (about 70, 60 or 50). In Pre-Lent we are being encouraged to go on this journey with Jesus for the perfecting of our knowledge of his passion and death and thus the renewal and deepening of our love. The images are of gardening in the first two Sundays – the parables of the Labourers in the Vineyard and of the Sower – calling us to attend to the garden that is our soul and our mission in the world. The Gospel for the final Sunday in Pre-Lent reveals the ignorance of the disciples about Christ's imminent passion and follows with Jesus' healing of a blind man who cries out to him in faith. The corresponding Epistles in Pre-Lent remind us of the prize of an incorruptible crown for which we restrain the flesh, encourage us to a Lenten discipline by the example

---

[12] This season changes in length depending on the date of Easter. But the final Gospels and Epistles are added to the end of Trinity season when Easter is early. They work in either location as the Gospels speak of Christ's final epiphany, when he returns to judge the quick and the dead, either to conclude Epiphany season or as the culmination of Trinity season and as a preparation for Advent; the Epistles reminding us that Christ has come to make us like himself for that day of judgement – wise, peaceful, loving, pure, righteous.

of St Paul, and direct us to charity, the character of and aim of entering into any spiritual discipline in Lent.

It has been suggested that the six Sundays in Lent can be divided into two main themes: the first three dealing with the hazards of the journey as we are confronted by conflicts with devils; the last three dealing with the end of our pilgrimage – the Jerusalem which is above which nourishes us, the increasing confrontation between truth and lies, concluding with the Passion of our Lord as we enter Holy Week. The corresponding Epistles encourage us to resist temptation and to seek the life of holiness, reminding us of our freedom in Christ and pointing us ever more clearly to the Cross. In Holy Week we read through the four Gospel accounts of the Passion of our Lord, trusting that in the very hearing of these accounts our souls will be changed.

Trinity Season – Our Sanctification

To understand the logic for the second half of the Church year, one must consider the time when the readings in the lectionary were chosen. It was developed soon after the time of St Augustine and of John Cassian. St Augustine had left to the Church a certain psychology of the soul and understanding of the soul's ascent to God.[13] John Cassian is important for bringing to the West the insights from the Eastern ascetics about the passions and our growth in the spiritual life in his *Conferences* and *Institutes*.[14] Whether or not the Anglican Reformers were aware of these teachings being embedded in the logic of the lectionary, by leaving the lectionary unchanged they have left these teachings about our soul and its sanctification for us to rediscover.[15]

---

[13] Especially in *Confessions* and *De Trinitate*.

[14] These works of Cassian, with one other, are the only texts listed specifically by name in the last chapter of the Rule of St Benedict (written in the seventh century) as further reading for those who would seek perfection.

[15] Some more recent commentators on the Trinity season lectionary in the Prayer Book have followed the misunderstanding that because of the way the lectionary developed, with dislocations of the propers originally

What follows is a suggestion that there is a more detailed logic for the choice of Epistles to go with the Gospel readings, beyond simply 'preserving relics of a course reading', and beyond what has been suggested in general terms about our sanctification in commentaries to date.

Stages in our growth in Holiness (Sanctification's length)
The early Church came to understand the spiritual life as characterized by three stages of growth in holiness – *purgation*, then *illumination* and leading to *union*.[16] The readings in Trinity season can be seen to reflect these three basic stages of spiritual growth, and in this order.

Purgation is a stage characterized by suffering as our lives are purged of sin, before we bear much fruit. Our suffering includes the pains of repentance (having to admit our failures); the pains inflicted by others who try to hold us back when

belonging together, that there is no real rationale for the ordering of Epistles and Gospels other than that 'the Epistles preserve relics of a course reading'. See, for example, M. H. Shepherd, *The Oxford American Prayer Book Commentary*, (New York, 1950) pp. 188–189. As noted above, this was the case with the lectionary preserved in the Roman Missal but is not the case with the Book of Common Prayer Eucharistic lectionary from the Sarum Missal, which preserved the lections largely unaltered from the Comes of St Jerome in the sixth century.

[16] Louth, Andrew, *The Origins of the Christian Mystical Tradition from Plato to Denys*, (Oxford, 1981), pp. 58, 102. At all times, in our life as Christians, these three stages are present. Even at the moment of our baptism, we were *purged* of sin, we began to be *illuminated* by the gift of the Spirit, and we were mystically *united* with Christ. Yet as we mature in our new life in Christ, as we are sanctified, there is a logical order in time of one stage before another. Our Lord cannot give to us spiritual gifts in abundance immediately or they will be misused by us, redirected to a destructive passion. The passions need to be reordered by grace – *purgation* first, then *illumination* (see Jas 4.1–3). As we come by grace to follow the Commandments and seek spiritual cleansing through Christ (*purgation*), our souls, like a polished mirror, reflect more fully the Divine life and we can see truth more clearly in our lives and when we read Scripture (*illumination*). As our souls are being *illuminated* by God, we are becoming *united* with Him in our lives – we think and desire and act more and more like Jesus.

we seek to reorder our lives to follow Christ; and the pains of self-control, described as the crucifying of the flesh (giving up bad habits). But this suffering is only the birth pains of the new virtuous life. We can find Bible passages in the Epistles that call us to this way of purgation in the Sunday readings from Trinity 3 (the Third Sunday after Trinity) to Trinity 9.[17] This call to bear with suffering in these Epistles would not be significant as characterizing a stage if there were references to suffering throughout the season, but they are not found as the main subject of a reading again in Trinity season.

Illumination is the stage characterized by the infilling of our souls with grace, with divine light – bringing truth, giving us inner spiritual strength, and blessing us with spiritual gifts. It is a call to the resurrection life, to rise to new life in the Spirit, and to seek the vision of God. These things are given greater focus in the Sunday readings from Trinity 10 to Trinity 16.[18] If you read through the Epistles you can see a remarkable shift in

[17] Trinity 3: *after that ye have suffered a while* (1 Pet. 5.5ff.).
Trinity 4: *the sufferings of this present time ... the whole creation groaneth and travaileth in pain* (Rom. 8.18ff.).
Trinity 5: *if ye suffer for righteousness' sake, happy are ye* (1 Pet. 3.8ff.).
Trinity 6: *our old man is crucified with him, that the body of sin might be destroyed* (Rom. 6.3ff.).
Trinity 7: Suffering is not referred to in Trinity 7 explicitly – but perhaps it is the suffering of spiritual weakness (Gospel – *they will faint by the way*) and of having given up sin but not yet redirecting that same love to God (Epistle).
Trinity 8: *if so be that we suffer with him* (Rom. 8.12ff.).
Trinity 9: *with the temptation* [he will] *also make a way to escape, that ye may be able to bear it* (1 Cor. 10.1ff.).
[18] Trinity 10: *Now there are diversities of gifts, but the same Spirit...But the manifestation of the Spirit is given to every man to profit withal* (1 Cor.12).
Trinity 11: *his grace which was bestowed upon me was not in vain* (1 Cor. 15) [Paul's vision of the risen Lord is a kind of illumination].
Trinity 12: *God hath made us able ministers of the new covenant; ...of the Spirit: ...how shall not the ministration of the Spirit be rather glorious?* (2 Cor. 3).
Trinity 13: The Epistle is a further reflection on the two Covenants; the Gospel begins, *Blessed are the eyes which see the things that ye see* (Lk. 10.23).

focus at Trinity 10. Doing a simple word count one finds only five references to the Spirit in the Sunday readings from Trinity 3 to 9 and only six references in Trinity 17 to 23. Compare this with 23 references to the Spirit in the Sunday readings from Trinity 10 to 16.

Union, the soul's ascension, is spoken about in the Bible in different ways. It includes the mystical marriage of the soul with God or of the Church with Christ; unity in our fellowship with our neighbour; the perfecting of the image of God in the soul; entering into God's rest; the contemplation of God; the vision of God. There are clear references to this end state of the soul in the Sunday readings from Trinity 17 to Trinity 23.[19]

Trinity 14: *Walk in the Spirit, and ye shall not fulfil the lust of the flesh... the fruit of the Spirit is... (Gal. 5.16f).*

Trinity 15: *If we live in the Spirit, let us also walk in the Spirit.... he that soweth to the Spirit shall of the Spirit reap life everlasting.* (Gal. 5.25f) [Note that this reference comes from the Epistle appointed in the Sarum Missal; it is the one Epistle that the Reformers replaced in Trinity season with Gal. 6.11–18].

Trinity 16: *I bow my knees unto the Father...that he would grant you...to be strengthened with might by his Spirit in the inner man (Eph. 3.16).*

[19] Trinity 17: *When thou art bidden of any man to a wedding, sit not down in the highest seat.* (Lk. 14) We are invited by our Lord to the mystical marriage of our soul with God. The union cannot be forced, at a certain stage in prayer we must simply wait in humility for God to lift us higher.

Trinity 18: *In every thing ye are enriched by him, in all utterance, and in all knowledge; even as the testimony of Christ was confirmed in you; so that ye come behind in no gift; waiting for the coming of our Lord Jesus Christ, who shall also confirm you unto the end* (1 Cor. 1.4ff.) This coming of the Lord Jesus is not the second coming. The Gospel speaks of knowing Christ not only as human but also as the Divine Son.

Trinity 19: *Be renewed in the spirit of your mind; and that ye put on the new man, which after God is created in righteousness and true holiness.* (Eph. 4.23) The focus of this Epistle is the clarification of the image of God in the soul. The original Epistle was Eph. 4.23–28, the Reformers added 6 verses before and 4 verses after, perhaps obscuring the original focus.

Trinity 20: *all things are ready: come unto the marriage.* (Mt. 22.1ff.) Our motivation for union with God (the mystical marriage) must be love: we must put on the marriage garment, put on Christ.

One can look at the three cycles of seven Sundays as relating to the classical medieval treatment of the soul's journey to God as one from being absorbed in the external world (carnally minded) (Trinity 3 to 9), to a movement within (Trinity 10–16), and finally to a movement above (spiritually minded) (Trinity 17–23). As the soul moves from the exterior to the interior to the superior, to a greater love of God, there is necessarily a corresponding greater love of neighbour – the reconciliation is both personal and social.

The emphasis of the Epistles and Gospels during these Sundays in Trinitytide shifts through these basic stages from purgation to illumination to union. But within those three stages, is there any particular reason for the ordering of the Sunday readings to help us in our growth?

The Passions of our Souls (Sanctification's breadth)
Early Christian monks (fourth and fifth century AD) studied carefully the various passions of the soul and their disorders. Their purpose was to help in the diagnosis of a soul's illnesses so that appropriate counsel could be given on how to overcome each vice, by grace. The 'seven deadly sins' come from this ancient tradition of summing up the disordered

Trinity 21: *Put on the whole armour of God, that ye may be able to stand against the wiles of the devil...and having done all, to stand.* (Eph. 6.10ff.) Is this call to endurance in prayer, to stand, a call to contemplation? The Gospel is the healing of a man's son who is at the point of death – an allegory of the inner man who is failing and in need of being restored (he besought Jesus that he would come down)?

Trinity 22: *Therefore is the kingdom of heaven likened unto a certain king which would take account of his servants.* (Mt. 18.21ff.) *He which hath begun a good work in you will perform it until the day of Jesus Christ...that you may be sincere and without offence till the day of Christ* (Phil. 1.3ff.).

Trinity 23: *For our conversation is in heaven; from whence also we look for the Saviour, the Lord Jesus Christ ... He will change our body that it may be fashioned like unto the body of His glory* (Phil. 3.17ff.) Whose is this image and superscription? ... *render unto God the things that are God's* (Mt. 22.15ff.). Our body is in the end in the likeness of Christ, a perfect instrument of love, and our soul in the image of the Trinity.

passions of the soul identified in the Bible by Jesus and his apostles[20] under certain categories, just as our medical profession gathers up diseases of the body under various categories, such as diabetes or cancer or heart disease.[21] The idea is that every disordered passion falls into one of these main categories. One early list considered eight disordered passions of the soul (from Evagrius of Pontus and brought to the West by John Cassian): gluttony, fornication, covetousness, wrath, dejection (meaning grief or sorrow), accidie or sloth, vainglory and pride (seen as the source of all the others).

The Bible readings in the first part of the season of Trinity may have been chosen to deal with these disordered passions (and their corresponding virtues, shown in brackets below) identified by early Christian psychologists in the following order:[22]

- Trinity 3 – Pride (Humility)
- Trinity 4 – Vainglory/Envy (True glory)
- Trinity 5 – Dejection or sorrow (Courage/Hope)
- Trinity 6 – Anger or wrath (Righteous anger/Forgiveness)
- Trinity 7 – Accidie or sloth (Zeal)

[20] See lists of disordered passions from Jesus in Mk. 7.20–23 and Mt. 15.18–20; and compare them with lists in the writings of St Paul in Rom. 1.29–31, Gal. 5.19–26, Eph. 4.17–6 and Col. 2.10–3; of St James in Jas 3.13–5.12; and of St Peter in 1 Pet. 2.11–4.19 and 2 Pet. 2–3.

[21] There are Scriptural grounds for wanting to identify seven or eight categories of disordered passions. Seven is a number used throughout the Bible to describe fullness. See also, for example, Mt. 12.43–45; Lk. 8.2; Prov, 26.24–26; and a spiritual reading of Deut. 7.1: the seven enemies of Israel in the promised land plus Egypt equals eight, seen as figures of the temptations we face in this life.

[22] There is a spiritual logic to the passions being dealt with in this order: the first two passions related to the rational aspect of the soul, the next three related to the irascible aspect, and the final two related to the appetitive aspect; these three aspects being a good description of the 'outer man'. (The passions are dealt with in a very similar order by Dante in the *Purgatorio* of the *Divine Comedy*, written in the fourteenth century, eight centuries after the lectionary.)

- Trinity 8 – Covetousness (Heavenly avarice)
- Trinity 9 – Gluttony and Fornication (Moderation)

The appointed Bible readings warn us of the various disorders and also give practical advice on how to be healed of them by Word and Sacrament.

The latter two series of seven Sundays (Trinity 10–16 and Trinity 17–23) may be dealing with these similar disorders and in the same pattern as in the first series, but in the context of the changed circumstances of the more spiritually mature Christian. We are led from looking at our outward actions and passions (Trinity 3–9) to look more deeply into our souls to root out disordered love at its source in our thoughts (Trinity 10–16). Then we are led to the heights of perfection (Trinity 17–23). We move from dealing with the 'outer man' to the unlocking and transformation of the hidden 'inner man', that aspect of our soul made in the image and likeness of God.[23] We are encouraged at every stage with the particular promises of God and the blessings, the gifts, the virtues, poured out on our souls as we grow in Christ.

The three Sundays at the beginning of Trinity season may act as an introduction to the season: showing us the beginning and end of our life in Christ (Trinity Sunday), and that it is all about the perfecting of our love and fear and encouraging us to enter upon this spiritual ascent (Trinity 1 and 2).

If this suggested rationale is correct, the Church has very carefully selected the Epistle and Gospel readings, so that the light of God's Word can be brought to shine in all its fullness on every part of the disordered and sanctified soul and at each stage of maturity in the Christian's life. The Sunday

[23] In St Augustine's *De Trinitate*, it is only the highest aspect of the rational soul that is a proper image and likeness of the Triune God. At this point we are beyond being driven by disordered passions, but not beyond imperfections in our knowing (Trinity 17 and 18) and willing (Trinity 19 to 21) and so our loving.

Eucharistic lectionary during Trinity season may cover in a very comprehensive and ordered way the *length* and *breadth* of our sanctification, our growth in holiness. The hope is that as the faithful read and hear this lectionary preached year after year and seek to follow its teaching more closely each time they are led to full Christian maturity.[24]

The Holy Days Eucharistic Lectionary
Throughout the Church year, the calendar has special days set apart as holy. The purpose of Holy Days, according to St Augustine, is to "dedicate and sanctify to God the memory of his benefits, lest unthankfulness and forgetfulness thereof should creep upon us in the course of time."[25] Whereas the Sunday readings through the Church year are about the faith that *justifies* and the life of *sanctification*, the Holy days lectionary has been seen as relating to our *glorification* in Christ.

> The rest of the days and times [holy days not directly related to our Lord] which we celebrate have relation all unto one head ... Forasmuch as we know that Christ hath not only been manifested great in himself, but great in other his Saints also, ...there are annual selected times to meditate of Christ glorified in them. [26]

In observing Holy days we grow in thankfulness as we reflect on and are encouraged and inspired by particular events in the life of Jesus and the examples of his followers who have embodied his grace in unique ways.

---

[24] There is a parallel to this idea of yearly reading of our spiritual ascent in the Orthodox monastic tradition, where St John Climacus' *Ladder of Divine Ascent* is read publicly each year during Lent.

[25] Augustine quoted by Richard Hooker, *Ecclesiastical Polity and other works by and about Mr Richard Hooker as collected by Mr. John Keble and revised by the Very Reverend R. W. Church and the Right Reverend F. Paget*, (facsimile reprint by Via Media Inc., Elliot City, Maryland, 1994) Book V, chapter LXX, p. 388.

[26] Hooker, ibid, p. 384

The location of some of the Holy Days in the Church year are related to high feast days such as Christmas and Easter. The location of the rest of the Saints days throughout the year needs further reflection, but one is often led to the conclusion that they are appointed to draw out and magnify the teaching presented in the Sunday Eucharistic lections that are close by in the Church year.

Conclusion

The 1662 Book of Common Prayer through its lectionaries promotes a comprehensive meditation on the life of Christ, so vast that we cannot see it all at once. These lectionaries set out a spiritual discipline for clergy and lay people alike to help lead us to that full vision of God.

In its present form it is a very ambitious plan for the reading of the whole of the Old Testament once a year, the New Testament twice, the Psalter twelve times, and for the hearing of the key passages in the Gospels and Epistles chosen by the early Church. We might conclude that it is too ambitious a plan, considering the few who continue to follow it. But for those wishing a rich and hearty well-ordered feast, the Prayer Book lectionaries set forth a banquet second to none. And for the health and salvation of souls surely we must ask: Have the modern lectionaries, which are less demanding and dangerously selective, really led this generation to greater biblical literacy? Is it not a form of despair that would conclude it is too much to commend to clergy and laity a pattern of 10 to 15 minutes of daily reading from 'that fountain and Well of truth'?

These lectionaries – the Eucharistic, Daily and Sunday Office, and Psalter – together teach us about the faith that justifies, our sanctification and Christ glorified in his saints. This ordered reading of the Bible is intended to immerse Anglicans in the images and stories of Scripture, to liberate and lead us to rest in the saving doctrine it teaches and to enflame our hearts with the love of God and our neighbour.[27]

The Eucharistic lectionary for Sundays and Holy Days, which the other lectionaries over time have come to support and enrich, has received scant attention in the Communion and we have almost allowed it to 'pass away as in a dream'. [28] But a careful study, with the assumption that there is a logic, has in the past and is beginning again to bear fruit in a recovery of the riches of a way of reading Scripture and the Church's teaching on Christian psychology and the spiritual ascent. It is hoped that the fruits of this recovery will begin to be known more fully in our lives and shared more widely within the Communion. In God's providence, it may also be one of those hidden treasures held onto by Anglicans through the centuries of our life apart that we can now offer back as a gift to the wider Church.

---

[27] As the Preface to the Prayer Book puts it, 'that the people (by daily hearing of holy Scripture read in the Church) might continually profit more and more in the knowledge of God, and be the more inflamed with the love of his true religion'.

[28] Richard Hooker, *The Laws of Ecclesiastical polity*, Works, Vol. I, ed. J. Keble (Oxford, 1841), p. 126; and see p. 20. This quotation is from Fr Curry's paper, 'Doctrinal Instrument of Salvation': see Part III.

The Book of Common Prayer in a Mixed Liturgical Economy

Peter Moger

The Revd Canon Peter Moger read Music at Merton College, Oxford and, after postgraduate study in composition, taught music in Sussex. He read Theology and trained for ordination at St John's College, Durham and was Curate at Whitby. After serving as Precentor of Ely and Vicar of Godmanchester, he was appointed National Worship Development Officer for the Church of England and subsequently Secretary of the Liturgical Commission. He is currently Canon Precentor of York Minster. He is the author of Crafting Common Worship *(Church House Publishing, 2009), co-editor of* Worship Changes Lives *(Church House Publishing, 2007) and a contributor of words and music to many publications for the Royal School of Church Music.*

The Book of Common Prayer is still the only form of Anglican liturgy directly authorized by Parliament and ... as one of the historic formularies of the Church of England, [is] doctrinally normative ... in a more immediate way than other liturgical forms.[1]

This quotation, from the Liturgical Commission's 2007 Report *Transforming Worship*, bears witness to the enduring place of

[1] *Transforming Worship: Living the New Creation*, A Report by the Liturgical Commission (2007), London: Church House Publishing.

the Book of Common Prayer within the life of the Church of England. Anglicans have traditionally expressed their theology through their liturgy: the two go hand in hand. A newly licensed priest, in making the Declaration of Assent, affirms his or her loyalty to the Anglican 'inheritance of faith' which includes the BCP (Book of Common Prayer). And when new liturgical material is debated prior to authorization by the General Synod, the BCP is inevitably cited as a touchstone of theological orthodoxy.[2]

Yet Prayer Book liturgical use is far from universal, and in the Church of England there are many worshippers who never encounter the Prayer Book and ministers who never use it. While this might be so, there is a case to be made for greater familiarity with the BCP, its contents and its tradition, as part of a truly vibrant mixed liturgical economy.

Liturgical Revision

For many generations the Church of England enjoyed a period of considerable liturgical stability. Apart from minor amendments to the BCP, the liturgy remained largely fixed from 1662 until well into the twentieth century, and the 1662 book was the only authorized provision for worship for 300 years. A single liturgy, though, has never prescribed a uniformity of theological approach or a monochrome liturgical practice: much of the genius of the 1662 book lies in the way in which it balances insights both Catholic and Reformed and is open to a range of interpretations. At the turn of the twentieth century, an Evangelical parish and a Catholic parish might have used the same words for the celebration of Holy Communion but they would have done so in ways that expressed clearly the distinctiveness of their respective traditions.

---

[2] The doctrine contained in The Book of Common Prayer and Administration of the Sacraments and other Rites and Ceremonies of the Church according to the Use of the Church of England is agreeable to the Word of God. (Canon A 3, 'Of The Book of Common Prayer', in *The Canons of the Church of England* 6th edition (2000), London: Church House Publishing).

A degree of latitude was allowed by the Act of Uniformity Amendment Act (Shortened Services Act) of 1872, one of the provisions of which was to enable the holding of services in addition to those in the BCP. The experience of service chaplains in the First World War exposed the need for greater flexibility than the Prayer Book afforded and this, along with other liturgical developments, led to a revision of the BCP, proposed – but not authorized by Parliament – in 1928. Despite many churches choosing to use the unauthorized 1928 Prayer Book, up until the 1960s, the Church of England still had what was essentially a single use: the 1928 book was a version of the BCP, and not an alternative to it.

The mid-twentieth century saw the rise of the liturgical movement, and with it a growth in prominence of the Parish Communion as the main Sunday act of worship. Liturgical revision became the order of the day in all the mainstream churches, leading in the Church of England to the first 'Alternative Services' of the 1960s and 70s. At first, these were light revisions of the Prayer Book text, but then – in the case of Alterative Services, Series 2 and 3 – came rites which differed markedly from the BCP in terms of structure (Series 2) and language (Series 3). The use of contemporary language, first seen in Series 3, marked another new departure for Anglican worship, mirroring the use of the modern vernacular in the Roman Catholic Church following the Second Vatican Council.

The Alternative Service Book 1980 (ASB) drew together the fruits of this new thinking and offered a collection of liturgy markedly different from that of the inherited Anglican use. Although clearly designed as an alternative to the BCP, there was some degree of continuity:

- Traditional language was preserved in Holy Communion Rite B;
- The Order for Holy Communion Rite A allowed for elements of the service to be used 'following the pattern of the Book of Common Prayer';

- The modern language orders for Morning and Evening Prayer were revised only in terms of their language: the structure was still very much that of the BCP;
- The use of BCP versions of Canticles (printed within the book) was permitted as an alternative to the ASB texts at Morning and Evening Prayer, and the BCP versions of the Gloria, Creed, Intercession, Confession, Absolution and Lord's Prayer as an alternative to the texts in Holy Communion Rite B.

The ASB proved to be a marker along the way of liturgical revision and expansion, with the process continuing apace through the 1980s and 90s. Much of the material which followed the ASB was supplementary, offering Anglicans a seasonal variety[3] [4] which had been largely absent from the worship of previous generations.

The Book of Common Prayer within a Mixed Economy Church: Common Worship

With the launch in 2000 of Common Worship (CW) – a vast collection of liturgical material published over eight years – a new concept was born. Designed to meet the liturgical needs of a Church with a growing diversity of types and styles of worship, CW has been published not as a book, but as a series of resources, available in printed form and online. Unlike the ASB, it is not an alternative to the BCP, but a collection of material which sits alongside it and – most importantly – incorporates elements of Prayer Book liturgy within it. The conscious decision to mix 'treasures old and new' is to some extent a reflection of its age, and the postmodern approach of a 'pick and mix' culture, just as was the ASB a reflection of the 'modern' outlook of the 1970s.

---

[3] *Lent, Holy Week, Easter: Services and Prayers* (1986), Church House Publishing, SPCK, Cambridge University Press.
[4] *The Promise of His Glory: Services and Prayers for the Season from All Saints to Candlemas* (1991), Mowbray/Church House Publishing.

Within CW, there are three important strands from the Prayer Book tradition to be found which serve both to stress the importance of this tradition within the complete worshipping life of the Church of England, and to redress some of the starkness to be found in earlier revised texts. One such strand is the collection of BCP and traditional language services found there.

In the 'main volume':

- Morning Prayer from the BCP (page 62)
- Evening Prayer from the BCP (page 72)
- Night Prayer (Compline) in traditional language (page 88)
- Prayers from the BCP (page 107)
- The Litany from the BCP (page 115)
- Holy Communion Order One in traditional language (page 207)
- Holy Communion Order Two (using the BCP text and structure) (page 228)
- Collects and Post Communions in Traditional Language (page 448).

In Common Worship: Pastoral Services:

- A Form of Solemnization of Holy Matrimony [1928 / Series 1] (page 418)
- An Order for the Burial of the Dead [1928 / Series 1] (page 430)
- An Order for the Burial of a Child (page 447)
- The Penitential Psalms (page 452).

Another is the inclusion (of a greater number than in the ASB) of Collects based on Prayer Book originals and, in some cases,[5] the use of an adapted BCP Collect as a Post Communion.

A third strand, less quantifiable, but discernable nonetheless, is the concern to restore to contemporary liturgy some of the

---

[5] e.g. The Post Communion for the Second Sunday of Lent, which is a contemporary language version of the BCP Collect for that Sunday.

poetry for which the BCP is justly prized, in contrast to the more prosaic style of the ASB. This can perhaps be seen most clearly in some of the newly composed extended eucharistic prefaces which exhibit a richness of imagery and Biblical reference and which strike a chord with the Prayer Book tradition.[6]

The inclusion of these elements within CW is a clear indication that the Church of England continues to value a living Prayer Book tradition as part of a diverse pattern of liturgy[7] within a mixed economy church.

The current use of The Book of Common Prayer

The fears of many in the 1970s and 1980s that liturgical revision would force the BCP entirely out of use have proved to be largely unfounded. While there is undeniably less use of the Prayer Book than there was a generation ago, there are many instances of thriving Prayer Book worship today – both in churches which have made this a distinctive (even defining) element of their identity, and in those places which have sought to embrace a genuine Anglican comprehensiveness. A glance at the Prayer Book Society's online list of churches where Prayer Book worship is offered,[8] gives a helpful overview of the current use of the BCP within the Church of England.

Parishes

In most parish churches which hold BCP services, the book is most commonly in use at said early morning Sunday celebrations of Holy Communion. Prayer Book Evensong continues in some parishes, typically in those places which maintain a choir and where there is a concern to keep alive the tradition

---

[6] An example might be the extended preface for Ordinary Time (Main volume, p. 294).

[7] This was underlined by the Liturgical Commission's statement that 'It is important that the Prayer Book remains in widespread and regular use in the mixed liturgical economy of the present-day church.' *Transforming Worship*, op. cit., 6.1.1.

[8] To be found on the Prayer Book Society's website, http://www.pbs.org.uk

of Anglican chant. BCP Matins is most common in rural areas, where sometimes, as part of a multi-parish benefice, it has become a lay-led service as part of a varied monthly pattern. Among the pastoral offices, the Marriage Service (albeit normally in its 1928 form) is widely used, and the Prayer Book funeral rite (also frequently the 1928 version) makes some occasional appearances (though these are declining). Baptism and Confirmation are generally seldom administered according to the BCP rite, though some bishops have made it known that they are happy to conduct BCP Confirmations if requested. There have continued to be occasional uses of the Ordination rites in recent years (though these have tended to be smaller services at which a single deacon or priest is ordained rather than large-scale diocesan occasions). There have been few consecrations to the episcopate using the BCP rite in recent years.[9]

Cathedrals

In cathedrals, greater churches and collegiate chapels, Prayer Book worship is generally strong, with the principal focus being Choral Evensong. In some places this attracts large congregations across a wide age range, forming part of the pattern of significant growth in cathedral attendances since the Millennium. Some cathedrals follow Cranmer's Psalm cycle, with the Psalms sung 'in course' throughout the month. In some foundations this is adhered to rigidly, even to the extent of ignoring 'proper' provision for Festivals. In other cathedrals, an amended scheme is used – sometimes in conjunction with the recently authorized Additional Weekday Lectionary (2010). Though weekday Choral Matins has now almost completely disappeared, on Sundays, Choral Matins continues to thrive in some cathedrals, though congregational numbers are often smaller than those attending the main Sunday Eucharist. Prayer Book services of Holy Communion

[9] The last one in the Church of England was the consecration of Richard Chartres as Bishop of Stepney in 1992.

in cathedrals range from simple said celebrations to solemn choral celebrations, though it is fair to say that the default setting for almost all Eucharistic worship in cathedrals is now Common Worship Order One in contemporary language.

What is clear is that, in many places of worship, the proportion of the BCP in regular liturgical use is usually relatively small – often only the orders for Holy Communion or Evening Prayer. A suggestion has been made that parish churches with an established tradition of BCP use might be encouraged to use as wide a range of BCP provision as possible (including the pastoral offices), in order to showcase the Prayer Book as a living resource within the full pastoral and worshipping life of a twenty-first century parish.[10]

The Book of Common Prayer and Training for Ministry
Given the enduring place of the BCP within the liturgical life of the Church of England, and its importance as a foundation of Anglican theology and polity, it is vital that those who prepare for ordained and lay ministry are given adequate training in Prayer Book practice. In addition to an historical under-standing of the theological and liturgical background to the BCP, ordinands and readers in training should be familiar with its content, whether or not they see themselves using it on a regular basis. The increasing flexibility of patterns of ministry now means that clergy and readers who might formerly have exercised their ministry exclusively within one tradition (or location) will now find themselves called upon to work across the old boundaries and to be competent in leading worship in traditions and contexts other than their own.

It is often hard, though, for those in training to gain the necessary experience to become familiar with Prayer Book worship. The vast majority of ordinands and readers in training are drawn from churches where the BCP has at most a small place in the scheme of worship, and many will have had no exposure to it at all prior to their selection for training.

[10] *Transforming Worship*, op. cit., 6.1.2.

IME 1–3

This therefore places a considerable responsibility on the part of Colleges, Courses and Schemes – as providers of theological education for Initial Ministerial Education (IME) 1–3[11] – to help make good this lack of experience of the BCP.

Reporting to the General Synod in 2007, the Liturgical Commission recommended

> ... that those preparing for ordained and licensed ministry should be given consistent exposure to the BCP, and should be grounded in its historical and theological context.[12]

The key here is that those in training are given 'consistent' exposure to the BCP *as worshippers*. Theological colleges can be well-placed to help here by using the BCP in their worship for extended periods of time, perhaps throughout the whole or part of a college term or a liturgical season. Consistent exposure is, of course, far more difficult to achieve for those training on regional courses or diocesan schemes, where corporate worship is a more occasional occurrence and where, in an ecumenical context, Anglican liturgy might be only part of a bigger picture. In these cases, judicious use of training placements within IME 1–3 might need to be made to ensure familiarity with Prayer Book worship for those without the necessary background.

All this assumes that those involved in delivering the training have themselves a working knowledge of the BCP – and a desire to equip others in its use – something which cannot necessarily be taken for granted. The recent demise of dedicated posts for the teaching of liturgy in theological training institutions has meant that this problem is likely to be further compounded.

---

[11] IME 1–3 is taken to mean the years of training prior to ordination to the diaconate, or licensing as a Reader.
[12] *Transforming Worship*, op. cit., 6.1.4.

IME 4–7

If IME 1–3 might help provide valuable experience of Prayer Book worship, then the need in IME 4–7[13] is to provide opportunities for presidential use of the BCP rites. It is ultimately the responsibility of training incumbents to ensure that those moving on from IME 4–7 to first incumbencies have had at least some experience of leading the main Prayer Book liturgies, though this could helpfully be reinforced by ensuring that BCP presidency features on the list of liturgical competencies required by diocesan training teams. Inevitably, for some curates and newly licensed Readers, practical experience will mean making use of parishes other than their own training parish in order to gain the necessary experience. A potential role for the Prayer Book Society might be seen here: in offering to broker links with parishes (or cathedrals) where BCP use is valued, and where an experienced minister might provide helpful training in its use.

It would also be helpful for specific guidance to be given on which 'BCP competencies' might reasonably be expected of the recently ordained / licensed by the end of IME 4–7. A suggestion might be:

- A working knowledge of those Prayer Book rites most commonly in use:
  - Holy Communion
  - Morning and Evening Prayer
  - Holy Matrimony (1928 Rite)
- The Burial Service (and how to adapt for use at a crematorium)
- A familiarity with the layout and contents of the book and where some of the 'gems' are to be found, e.g, the General Thanksgiving, the State Prayers, the Litany, the Prayer for all sorts and conditions of men.

---

[13] IME 4–7 equates to the time spent in a curacy, or the first four years of licensed Reader ministry.

The recent posting of the entire text of the BCP on the Church of England website (achieved with the financial support of the Prayer Book Society) is a valuable tool here, offering a clear overview of the contents, and an easily navigable and reliable text.

In some dioceses, Eucharistic presidency is taught as part of a diocesan IME programme in Year 4, in the months immediately before ordination to the priesthood. If this is the case, it is vital that presidency at the BCP rite is included as part of the programme.[14]

In all the work of training for ordained and licensed ministry, the concept of partnership is key. Regional Training Partnerships, set up in the past five years, offer formal structures within which diocesan training teams, courses, schemes and colleges may collaborate and share resources. The potential for diocesan worship committees, the *Praxis* regions,[15] and the Prayer Book Society to be involved within these partnerships is considerable, and is absolutely crucial if steps are to be taken to remedy the current lack of training in BCP worship. Only in this way will the Prayer Book continue to thrive as a living part of the rich and varied tapestry of Church of England worship.

---

[14] As in the excellent Eucharistic presidency training offered by Sheffield Diocesan Liturgical Committee as part of the IME 4–7 programme.
[15] *Praxis*, a collaborative venture of the Liturgical Commission, the Alcuin Club and the Group for the Renewal of Worship, was set up in 1990 to enable liturgical formation throughout the country. Organised on a regional basis, it offers day conferences and training materials designed to enrich and resource worship of all traditions within the Church of England.

Section 4

Mission and the Book of Common Prayer

1662 – Our Evangelical Future?

C. Peter Molloy

The Revd C. Peter Molloy is the Rector of the Lakes & Locks Parish in the Diocese of Ontario, Canada and is the Editor-in-Chief of The Anglican Planet, *the largest independent newspaper within in the Anglican Church of Canada, and has contributed to various Church publications. He studied at Carleton University, the University of British Columbia and Regent College. He lives in Westport, Ontario with his wife Ann.*

In the year 2000, I was ordained and set off to minister in a small northern Saskatchewan parish. Being a relatively recent convert to Anglicanism, having been raised and nurtured in both Baptist and Methodist traditions, I was quite excited to join a faithful, lively and intelligent college of priests, hoping that their experience would supplement my short Anglican history. As I began to meet the other clergy of the diocese, slowly my mother's words began coming back to me as I began realise once again that I am 'not exceptional'. Among them, I found converts to Anglicanism from a wide range of churches: Pentecostal, Brethren, Mennonite, Charismatic, Lutheran; all having left the church of their youth and walking the Canterbury trail, as it were.

Common to many of us was a deep dissatisfaction with the theology and liturgy of the traditions in which we were raised. The particular hook upon which I was caught and reeled into Anglicanism was the Book of Common Prayer. Perhaps it was the novelty of this new-found treasure that caused me to cherish it so, but I really think it was more than that.

Having grown up in an Evangelical home and church, I often find old friends and family are curious about 'why I switched'. I am always pleased to respond that in Anglicanism, by which I really mean within the Book of Common Prayer, I have found a much more robust Evangelicalism. Becoming an Anglican was not so much a rejection of the Evangelical convictions I was raised on, but rather finding a tradition which more effectively promotes them. Evangelicals who hold dear the priorities the authority of Scripture, the need for conversion and a liturgy and theology which centres on Christ Jesus' atoning act on the Cross, should find in the Book of Common Prayer a living tradition which will guard and nurture their ministry. The Book of Common Prayer, through the effective way in which these central Christian tenets are promulgated, is a great light which can bring doctrinal clarity within the church and Gospel clarity within the world. Evangelicals would do well to recommit themselves to the Prayer Book way.

Let us consider how these Evangelical concerns are promoted through the Book of Common Prayer.

Devote Yourself to the Public Reading of Scripture ...
The church is not always given to subtlety, and the theological priorities of a given institution are usually fairly easy to discern from its name or motto. St John's College, Nottingham, for instance, uses 'Woe to me if I do not preach the gospel'.[1] Wycliffe Hall, Oxford, named after the great English translator, uses the motto, '*Via, Veritas, Vita*': the Way, the Truth and the Life.[2] Its colonial counterpart, Wycliffe College, Toronto, claims for itself '*Verbum Domini manet*': The Word of the Lord Endures.[3] The message is clear: we Evangelicals

[1] 1 Cor. 9.16.
[2] Jn. 14.6.
[3] Pet. 1.25.

are Bible Christians. Anglo-Catholics may have their traditions, and the Charismatics may have the Holy Spirit, but
Evangelicals stand firm on the Word of God. It might sound
far-fetched, but it is even possible that this can be a source of
spiritual pride for Evangelicals.

These distinctions are, of course, a matter of emphasis.
I remember a conversation with a senior and godly Anglo-
Catholic priest one afternoon at my first clergy retreat. I was
raising the Evangelical flag at every opportunity, and so he
kindly asked me to describe what distinguished Evangelicals.
With great pride I explained that 'we uphold the authority of
God's Holy Word'. He quite charitably mused that he had
never been aware that he did otherwise, and proceeded to lead
us in Evening Prayer.

That being said, Evangelicals do place a distinct emphasis
on the unique authority of Scripture and confidence in its
transforming power, and we should take particular care that
our liturgy reflects that. Paul writes in his second letter to
Timothy: 'All Scripture is breathed out by God and profitable
for teaching, for reproof, for correction, and for training
in righteousness, that the man of God may be competent,
equipped for every good work'.[4] This is one of the founda-
tional passages for the Evangelical belief that Scripture has a
transforming effect, that through the grace of the Holy Spirit,
the Word of God changes hearts and minds for the daily
battle of living a life of godliness and furthering the Kingdom
of God. To this end Paul reminds Timothy that his duty as
a Christian leader is to keep Scripture before the eyes of the
fledgling body under his charge and so he writes, 'Until I come,
devote yourself to the public reading of Scripture, to exhortation, to teaching'.[5] For Evangelicals, then, the Prayer Book
should be regarded as a gift of great value as it simply is the
Bible re-arranged for public worship. Regardless of whatever

[4] 2 Tim. 3.16–17 (Unless otherwise indicated all quotations in this
essay are taken from the English Standard Version).
[5] 1 Tim. 4.13.

other challenges a parish might face, the Prayer Book keeps Scripture before their eyes.

I never grow tired of hearing visitors from other Evangelical churches remark, usually with some surprise, how biblical they found our service to be. By this they usually mean the amount of Scripture they heard read, how they were invited to praise God through the words of Scripture in the Psalms and the Canticles, and the comprehensive and fundamentally biblical nature of prayer. Perhaps they would also have noted how the Book of Common Prayer justifies its every movement through relevant Scripture sentences, and hopefully they will have discerned that the standpoint of the preaching was one of faithfully applying the Scriptures appointed for the day. This is the great gift of the Prayer Book: it reads Scripture, offers praise through Scripture, prays scriptural concerns, and stands under the authority of Scripture – and that should warm the hearts of all Evangelicals.

This fundamental biblical characteristic is observed frequently when the Book of Common Prayer is discussed, but we should not let our familiarity with this rare treasure diminish our appreciation of it. The Prayer Book's unique scriptural pattern of worship is not to be found in such fullness elsewhere. In modern Anglican liturgies, it is not the lack of beauty in the language, or the loss of the historic character of the liturgy that is their great failing (although these are both enormous losses): what we should lament most is the paucity of scriptural content and of a fundamentally scriptural character to our worship.

Other Reformed Churches make great use of Scripture, usually the recitation of the Psalms and Scripture readings, but usually not the fullness of the canticles and prescribed, scripturally formed prayers. When we look at non-liturgical Evangelical churches, while the teaching can often be thoroughly scriptural, the role of Scripture elsewhere in the service is quite limited. Perhaps it is read independent of the sermon, and usually scripture sentiments or phrases are alluded to in a praise song, but often Scripture is relegated to isolated verses which buttress the homiletical journey of the pastor. It is easy to see why John Wesley was justified in concluding that there is 'no Liturgy in the world, either in ancient or modern language, which breathes more of a solid, scriptural, rational piety than the Common Prayer of the Church of England'.[6] How can Evangelicals, who see how formative public worship is, jettison such a biblical form?[7]

What is true of the public worship in the Book of Common Prayer is even truer of the pattern of private worship to which the Prayer Book invites all Christians. Here are to be found all of the same elements, the canticles and the biblical model of prayer in the Daily Office. But what we find in even greater measure is the priority of a comprehensive reading of Scripture. The Book of Common Prayer Daily Office lectionary encompasses a most rigorous pattern of Scripture reading. If you followed the Daily Office lectionary over the course of a year, the Old Testament would be read once, the New Testament twice, and the Psalms 12 times. Again, I suspect this observation is not new to readers of this volume, but it is nonetheless a remarkable gift, and enormously formative for any who follow this pattern.

Of course, liturgy should not be simply measured by the percentage of Scripture it contains, any more than whisky should be judged simply on its percentage of alcohol. If there is some hope of either having effect, however, we would do well to look for high content in its most potent ingredient. That being said, there are other qualities that should be considered, and here we see the Book of Common Prayer moving from strength to strength.

---

[6] From the Preface of *The Sunday Services of the Methodists in the United States of America with other Occasional Services* (1790).

[7] It is worth noting that Christian formation is not the only, or even the first, priority of public worship. But it is often on the grounds that 'people cannot get anything out of language they do not understand' that the Book of Common Prayer is rejected. If we recognise that the primary purpose of worship is the glorification of God, then this argument against the Prayer Book appears much weaker.

Simul Justus et Peccator

Another point of emphasis in Evangelicalism is the need for conversion of heart. That is, we recognise that the Christian life requires a turning away from old patterns of sin and the concerns of this world; we see this clearly in the Book of Common Prayer.

I often hear jibes from my evangelical friends of other denominations that Anglicans let people 'get away with a lot', that perhaps we do not require people to repent and turn from their sins – and that it can be a pretty comfortable place for people to remain unchallenged. I ask in response whether they have ever been to a service where the Book of Common Prayer is employed. We find throughout the Prayer Book the challenge to live a life of repentance.

'Repent Ye for the Kingdom of God is at hand'[8] ushers in the Christian Year in the Daily Office. The Baptismal service requires a renunciation of 'the devil and all his works, the vain pomp and glory of the world, with all covetous desires of the same, and the sinful desires of the flesh'. The Book of Common Prayer includes in every service a call to confession. The Daily Office invites us to 'confess our manifold sins and wickedness; and that we should not dissemble nor cloke them before the face of Almighty God our heavenly Father'. And then in our Holy Communion service all the communicants are gathered together in praying 'We do earnestly repent, And are heartily sorry for these our misdoings; The remembrance of them is grievous unto us; The burden of them is intolerable'. It is hard to imagine how one might be more clear in calling for repentance.

On the other hand, there are many within the church who feel that the Book of Common Prayer charts too penitential a course – keeping us too preoccupied with 'bewailing our manifold sins.' Wonderfully, however, we see that the Prayer Book does not leave us in such a miserable estate but, through the mercy of God, the Priest or Bishop is instructed

---

[8] Mt. 3.2 (Coverdale translation).

to pronounce these words: 'Have mercy upon you; pardon and deliver you from all your sins; confirm and strengthen you in all goodness; and bring you to everlasting life; through Jesus Christ our Lord.' We hear here the marvellous and gracious good news of having our sins forgiven. Not only that, however, as through the path of repentance and absolution we are also exhorted to move forward in faith. The absolution contains the sanctifying prayer that our repentance might be confirmed and strengthened by God, and made manifest in our growing in goodness: the very fruit of a true penitent heart, set free by Christ, to love as it ought. The daily repetition of this penitential pattern is a real strength in the Book of Common Prayer. It invites Christians into a life of conversion and renewed and increased conversion.

When I was a child, I attended a Methodist church camp which had evangelistic tent meetings each summer. It was the place where many of my siblings and I gave our hearts to the Lord. Now I was raised in a Christian home and cannot actually remember a time when I thought my heart belonged to anyone else. Yet, here at camp, I was invited each summer to turn away from sin and give my life to God, which I joyfully confess I did – several times each summer. I remember one year, as I was making my tearful journey to the altar rail, my cabin counsellor put his hand on my shoulder and suggested that I should return to my seat as I had 'already done that'. To be fair, I had, in his presence, 'done it' in previous years, and earlier that week. Yet stubbornly I pressed forward, because the words of the call were still true. I was still a sinner and I wanted to repent and know forgiveness. I fear that yet another letter on the subject of my wilfulness was sent home to my parents.

It is, of course, not quite fair to contrast Thomas Cranmer's understanding of redemption and sanctification with that of a 15-year-old camp counsellor. However, when I came as an adult to embrace Anglicanism, it was essentially along these lines: that I found for the first time in the Book of

Common Prayer a pattern which took seriously my need for on-going conversion and repentance, a pattern that regarded conversion as a lifetime of slowly handing over more and more of my life, and not just a one-time event. Later on I discovered Luther's wonderful formula which describes Cranmer's approach so well: *Simul Justus Et Peccator*, that is, 'Righteous and at the same time a Sinner'. This is the genius of the Book of Common Prayer: not that we beat our chests as men without hope and wallow in our sin, but rather that in hopefulness we acknowledge our sin, receive grace and go forth in faith.

J. I. Packer sees this fundamentally evangelical pattern as being the central logic of the Book of Common Prayer. He writes:

> Cranmer saw that the way to make liturgy express the gospel is by use of a sequence of three themes. Theme one is the personal acknowledgment of sin; theme two is the applicatory announcement of God's mercy to sinners; theme three is the response of faith to the grace that is being offered. The sequence is evangelical and edifying – edifying, indeed, just because it is evangelical. Gospel truth is what builds us up![9]

Surely this pattern, which sees the path to spiritual maturity through the recognition of both our offensive sin and God's redemptive grace, should be cherished by Evangelicals. The wonderful hymnody of the Wesleys, Newton and Cowper was saturated with this double knowledge of our wretchedness and God's grace. Hear Newton's glorious yet oft overlooked hymn 'Approach my Soul, the Mercy Seat':

[9] J. I. Packer (1996), 'For Truth, Unity and Hope: Revaluing the Book of Common Prayer', *The Machray Review* #58. The Machray Review was a Journal of the Prayer Book Society of Canada and is no longer published, but articles from past issues are available on line on the Prayer Book Society of Canada website, www.prayerbook.ca

Approach, my soul, the mercy seat,
  Where Jesus answers prayer;
There humbly fall before His feet,
  For none can perish there.

Bowed down beneath a load of sin,
  By Satan sorely pressed,
By war without and fears within,
  I come to Thee for rest.

O wondrous love! to bleed and die,
  To bear the cross and shame,
That guilty sinners, such as I,
  Might plead Thy gracious Name.

Similarly, one cannot help but see the marks of Cranmerian formation in the preaching of George Whitefield. His sermon 'Repentance and Conversion' reveals his recognition of the daily need to consider our simultaneous state of grace and sin as being necessary steps for growing in faith:

> O ye servants of the most high God, if any of you are here tonight, though I am the chief of sinners, and the least of all saints, suffer the word of exhortation. I am sure I preach feelingly now; God knows I seldom sleep after three in the morning; I pray every morning, Lord, convert me, and make me more a new creature today. I know I want to be converted from a thousand things, and from ten thousand more: Lord God, confirm me; Lord God, revive his work.[10]

C. S. Lewis in his splendid essay 'Miserable Offenders' defends this confessional clarity against the attack of modern self-affirming sentiment thus:

---

[10] *Whitefield's Sermon Outlines*, selected and edited by Sheldon B. Quincer (1956), Grand Rapids: W. B. Eerdmans, pp. 67–68.

A serious attempt to repent and really to know one's own sins is in the long run a lightening and relieving process. Of course, there is bound to be at first dismay and often terror and later great pain, yet that is much less in the long run than the anguish of a mass of unrepented and unexamined sins, lurking the background of our minds. It is the difference between the pain of the tooth about which you should go to the dentist, and the simple straight-forward pain which you know is getting less and less every moment when you have had the tooth out.[11]

What the Book of Common Prayer calls for, both explicitly in its liturgy and implicitly by encouraging all Christians to participate in the Daily Office, is a pattern of conversion and reconversion or increased conversion. While some might wish to move past this penitential moment and not dwell on it, Packer upholds this as a necessary part of our sanctification process and describes the re-treading of this ground as the tightening of the screw. The effect of this sanctifying pattern is that through faith and the daily recognition that we are sinners in need of repentance, God's grace is known more and more to us as Christ Jesus' victory is increased more and more in our lives and in his Church. This brings us to our final point.

But we preach Christ crucified ...

Finally we turn to the Evangelical plank of Crucicentrism or the centrality of Christ and his atoning work on the Cross. The difficulty here is not in finding evidence of Cranmer's Crucicentrism, but rather it is in selecting only a few examples. It is no exaggeration to say that you can barely open a page of the Book of Common Prayer which does not encourage the one praying implicitly or explicitly to put his or her hope in Christ alone. The Eucharistic lections point again and again to Christ's salvific work. The Daily Office encourages us to

[11] C. S. Lewis, 'Miserable Offenders' in *God in the Dock*, published in *The Collected Works of C.S. Lewis (1996)*, Eerdmans, p. 384.

bring our everyday concerns before God in the effective name of Christ Jesus. Virtually all of the Prayer Book points us to that wonderful and unique truth that Christ died for our sins and invites us to put our confidence in him. Perhaps, though, it is in the service of Holy Communion that we find Cranmer going to the greatest lengths to make this point clear.

Other writers in this volume will give appropriate attention to Cranmer's unparalleled prose style and I will simply state that I agree wholeheartedly! I have found, though, that it is always important to take note of where Cranmer's melodic line stumbles or is strained, because usually here we will find an instance where Cranmer has refused to subordinate his theological commitments to prose style. There is such an example in the declaration at the beginning of the Prayer of Consecration, over which many a new or sleepy priest has faltered:

ALMIGHTY God, our heavenly Father, who of thy tender mercy didst give thine only Son Jesus Christ to suffer death upon the Cross for our redemption; *who made there (by his one oblation of himself once offered) a full, perfect, and sufficient sacrifice, oblation, and satisfaction, for the sins of the whole world*; and did institute, and in his holy Gospel command us to continue, a perpetual memory of that his precious death, until his coming again; ...

This formula, a Cranmer original introduced in 1549 and clarified even further in 1552, seems somewhat awkwardly inserted into the Prayer of Consecration. Cranmer here takes great pains to insist on the absolute sufficiency of Christ's self-offering against the medieval theology of the Mass. Compare the above with the Gregorian Canon upon which Cranmer based much of his work. In the equivalent section in the Gregorian Canon, the *Te Igitur*, we see great weight placed on the effectiveness and worthiness of the Priest and the Church in making sacrifice:

> Most merciful Father, we humbly pray and beseech
> Thee, through Jesus Christ Thy Son, Our Lord, to accept
> and to bless these + gifts, these + presents, these + holy
> unspotted Sacrifices, which we offer up to Thee, in the
> first place, for Thy Holy Catholic Church, that it may
> please Thee to grant her peace, to preserve, unite, and
> govern her throughout the world; ...

It is this theology of the Mass which clouds the unique role
of Christ as a sinless mediator that Cranmer rejects in his
Prayer of Consecration. Interestingly, he does not give up
the language of satisfaction as other Reformers had done.
Instead he rightly attributes the completeness of this satisfaction to Christ Jesus' once-for-all sacrifice on the Cross.
In case we are inclined to miss it he underlines the point in
Article XXXI, *Of the one oblation of Christ finished upon
the Cross*:

> THE offering of Christ once made is the perfect
> redemption, propitiation, and satisfaction for all the
> sins of the whole world, both original and actual, *and
> there is none other satisfaction for sin but that alone.*
> Wherefore the sacrifices of Masses, in the which it was
> commonly said that the priests did offer Christ for the
> quick and the dead to have remission of pain or guilt,
> were blasphemous fables and dangerous deceits.

Article XXXI and its substantial manifestation in the Prayer
of Consecration were the sharp end of the stick for Cranmer's
Reformed assertion of the salvific uniqueness of Christ. As
Ashley Null puts it, 'The heart of Cranmer's solifidianism
was that salvation through any other means exalted man at
God's expense'.[12] Evangelical Anglicans in our day should
not be afraid to adhere to Cranmer's clear liturgy in our

[12] Ashley Null (2000), *Thomas Cranmer's Doctrine of Repentance:
Renewing the Power to Love*, Oxford University Press, p. 245.

contemporary attempts to assert the uniqueness of Christ's once-for-all offering against the pernicious impulse of modern Anglicans to insert themselves into Christ's sacrifice.

Regrettably, the plethora of liturgical options available to contemporary Anglicans makes a line-by-line comparison virtually impossible, but suffice it to say that Cranmer's careful Crucicentrism is rarely maintained.[13] Looking at the modern rites in Common Worship, we see that the proximity of the Offering and the Prayer of Consecration has the effect of subtly conflating our offerings of the Eucharistic elements and our tithes with our Lord's once-for-all self-offering for the remission of sins. This is further enforced with misleading language which elevates our role and worthiness in the Eucharist through the offering of the gifts of Bread and Wine. We see one of many examples in Eucharistic Prayer B: 'As we offer you this our sacrifice of praise and thanksgiving, we bring you this bread and this cup and we thank you for counting us worthy to stand in your presence and serve you'. Compare this with Cranmer's insistence that even the Eucharistic elements are God's gift to us who through our sin have no claim to participate whatsoever: ' ... we receiving these thy creatures of bread and wine', and 'We are not worthy so much as to gather up the crumbs under thy table'. It is an effective reversal of what Cranmer took great pains to establish.[14]

---

[13] To be fair, Common Worship does provide optional Eucharistic rites which do attempt to maintain Cranmer's Crucicentric language, something which even the traditional language rite does not in Canadian Book of Alternative Services (1985). Reformed-minded Anglicans might appreciate this accommodation. The trouble, however, with Common Worship is not so much what is there, as what else is there. Rather than being a pattern for the public and private spiritual life of Anglican Christians as the Book of Common Prayer has been in the past, Common Worship exists as a resource book to allow for whatever liturgical tastes exist in any given parish. This cafeteria approach cannot effectively form a Church along the Evangelical lines that Cranmer held to be so important. Common Worship relegates Cranmer's careful Crucicentrism to the status of an option for 'those who like that sort of thing'.
[14] The reader perhaps might think that this is splitting hairs, but often this sort of careful attention to meaning is the difference between orthodoxy

Michael Green, in his essay 'New Testament Christianity
is Reflected Courageously in the Book of Common Prayer',
complains along similar lines that the modern Canadian rites
betray both the Prayer Book and New Testament Christianity
in that in the middle of each of the various options, they all say
'We offer you this bread and this cup ...'. The problem with
this, he writes, is that:

> ... I don't come to God in Holy Communion to tell Him
> what a fine fellow I am and to offer Him the bread and
> the cup. I'm not a fine fellow. I'm a deep-dyed sinner and
> I come to feed on that which makes alive and real to me
> His precious death for me. I come as a guest, who has no
> right even to be at that table except for His mercy. I am
> not worthy to pick up the crumbs under His table, were
> it not for His great mercy.
>   And I come on my knees as a sinner to Jesus, and it's
> wonderful. I don't come to offer Him the bread and the
> cup. I come to receive ... the fruit of Calvary. His body
> broken and His blood shed; only in response to that can
> I offer Him my poor self and service.[15]

This absolute Crucicentric clarity, which Cranmer insists upon
explicitly in the Prayer of Consecration and in Article XXXI
and which undergirds the rest of the Book of Common Prayer,
calls daily on all Christians, uniquely and finally to place all of
their hope in Christ Jesus and his work, on the Cross. This sort
of theological clarity is not found in other liturgies. Gregory
Dix regarded Cranmer's 1552 Book of Common Prayer as the
'only effective attempt ever made to give liturgical expression

and heresy (i.e. the difference between *Homoousios* and *Homoiousios*). It
is the duty of the parish priest to pay careful attention to such matters for
the sake of the parish. With the rise of Parish Communion Movement this
becomes even more important, as even slight distinctions repeated weekly
can be either formative or deformative.
[15] Michael Green (1996), 'New Testament Christianity is Reflected
Courageously in the Book of Common Prayer', *The Machray Review* #58.

to the doctrine of "justification by faith alone" '.[16] This life-giving doctrine which was a driving force of the English Reformation has been effectively obscured and marginalised by attempts to 'update the liturgy'. Evangelicals would do well to follow Cranmer's lead and not sacrifice doctrinal clarity for the sake of what they may perceive to be more pleasing form.

1662: Our Once and Future Prayer Book

It would be an understatement to say that twenty-first-century Anglicans face difficult times. Even if we could set aside for a moment the various differences which are straining the bonds of the Anglican Communion, we still face the enormous challenge of advancing the Gospel on the ground in parishes around the globe. In this there is a constant temptation for Evangelicals to jettison the Book of Common Prayer. The reasons for this are fairly straightforward. The Elizabethan language is antiquated and has the whiff of irrelevance, and in an era which cherishes free expression, the limited and prescribed responses of clergy and laity alike seem constrictive. And surely books themselves are a flat and obsolete technology in an age of PowerPoint and Kindles? With the parish church largely in decline, clergy and churches are anxious to 'do something' to revive interest in Christianity. Modernising liturgy is often seen as an easy, and frequently welcome, change. Yet at what cost?

Whatever short-term gains might be found in bringing in contemporary liturgies, this move almost certainly involves diminishing and distorting the clear Evangelical priorities which Cranmer set forth in 1552 and which were retained in the 1662 Book of Common Prayer. Regrettably, modern Anglicanism has set a greater priority on the style of the liturgy than on the substance. I am neither an historian nor a statistician, but it would seem that this impulse has not borne good fruit here in North America. And one cannot help but see how our distorted and ineffective Gospel witness relates immediately to a diminished view on these very issues that

---

[16] Dom Gregory Dix (1945), *The Shape of the Liturgy*, Dacre Press, p. 672.

Cranmer attempted to set right: the authority of Scripture, our need for conversion and the work of Christ on the Cross.

I would urge fellow Evangelicals and Anglicans generally, as we prayerfully consider the way forward, to give serious consideration to retaining and (where it has been lost) restoring the Book of Common Prayer. It is the very root of English Evangelicalism, and what greater need have we in our modern confusion than to find and be nourished by our roots once again?

What Really Drives Anglican Mission?[1]

George Sumner

The Revd Canon Dr George R. Sumner is the Principal of Wycliffe College, an evangelical and Anglican theological college in Toronto, Canada, where is he also Helliwell Professor of World Mission. He earned a PhD in systematic theology from Yale University. His books include The First and the Last, Being Salt, *and a commentary on Daniel (Brazos, forthcoming). He has served as a teacher at St. Philip's Theological College, Kongwa, and as a priest on a native reserve in Arizona, USA.*

We live in a time when the rhetoric of mission is much in vogue. This grows in part out of obedience to a central theme of the New Testament, but is also probably a response to the worrisome decline of the Church in numbers and prominence. Today the key terms of missiology (the study of mission) are deployed by liberals and conservatives of various kinds alike. We speak of the mission that belongs first to God himself, the *missio Dei*, in which we are invited to participate. Similarly we hear that Churches should be 'missional,' defined from

[1] The author appreciates the permission of the *Anglican Theological Review* (39:3) for permission to reprint this article, here adapted. Earlier versions were delivered to the Bishop Elliott Society in San Antonio, Texas in January 2006. A second version was offered as the Arnold Lecture of the Diocese of Nova Scotia in September 2006.

the outset by their mission to the world and not by their own concerns. Both are in a sense undeniably true, though different users fill out the terms with quite different content. Likewise everyone calls on the Church to be 'incarnational', that is, responsive to its own context, though again what this response should look like differs widely.[2] We worry that the terms become all-purpose warrants for what we were intending to do in ministry. Furthermore, the use of these terms does not assure a deep commitment to the proclamation of the Gospel, or self–sacrificial service, or, for that matter, the success of the ministry in question. We might well ask what are the conditions, in the community and in ourselves, which indicate the deeper and more fruitful applications of such ideas. Saying the words does not predict seriousness in mission – so what does? And along the way, we wonder what particular slant Anglicans might have on these questions.

The helpmate that missiology has traditionally used in its reflection is the social sciences, and we do well to turn to them for help at the outset. It should come as no great surprise, then, that one of the most insightful accounts of the dynamics of a successful missionary effort has been offered by the noted British sociologist David Martin, who is, incidentally, a traditional Anglican. His 1990 book *Tongues of Fire*[3] dealt with the dramatic growth of the Pentecostal church in Latin America. His account helps us tease out a more general theory of how mission tends actually to work:

It is easy to dismiss Latin American Pentecostals as displaying some of the least attractive features of commercialized North American evangelical missions:

---

[2] See for example H. H. Rosin's *Missio Dei: An Examination of the Origin, Contents. And Function of the Term in Protestant Missiological Discussion*, (Leiden: Interuniversity Institute, 1972).
[3] *Tongues of Fire: The Explosion of Pentecostalism in Latin America*, (Oxford: Blackwell, 1990).

they are theologically unsophisticated, shy away from political engagement even in repressive contexts, and retain a male–centered style of leadership. But Martin bids his readers look more closely. Immigrants to the cities found the warmth of their clans and the vivid social life of the fiesta, but in a new community that made possible new aspirations. Their tongues were loosed, their diseases cured, and the story they had heard in the village Catholic church became their own. They learned virtues of gentleness and mutuality in the home, so that a whole new style of maleness emerged, the real revolution, while still under the banner of male headship. All this could only happen in peaceable enclaves within the cracks of the old society, with its authoritarian solidarities of church and state. In these enclaves a new way of living according to the gospel could be imagined, and space found for it to germinate. Only later would this new life be let loose on the larger society for its gradual transformation.

Martin cites important historical precedents. Was it not so with the monasteries in the early medieval period, or with the communities of the *devotio moderna* in the late Middle Ages leading to the Reformation, or of the Quakers with their Christian dreams of abolition and suffrage? Did they not all first grow as cells in social worlds broken apart by the end of an epoch, or by the fragmentation of the modern age?

What Martin is describing, I want to name the 'dense encryptment' of the Christian belief and way as they dispersed into society in general, in what he calls the 'peaceable operation of cultural logic':

Primitive Christianity itself began as a movement active solely at the level of culture, and in this respect, as in many others, evangelical Christianity represents a return to this primitive condition. The contemporary evangelical in Latin America has walked out of the extant structures and devised an experimental capsule or cell in the

interstices of culture. Here he may reinvent himself in an
atmosphere of fraternal support and give 'tongue' to his
frustrations and aspirations. Induction into new worlds
and socialization into symbolic reversals may in time
become diffused into whole populations ... a mutation
in self–consciousness or skills in public address and
organization may be transferred into any other sphere
whatsoever ... they are protean in their potential.[4]

Christian mission, then, whatever the rhetoric may be, flour-
ishes where 'dense encryptment', the intense formation of belief,
ethics, social cohesion, and prayer, sufficient for combustion
into mission, may be found. If we consider the main arena
of this collection of essays, namely Anglicanism, it is clear
that for Anglicans the primary means of such encryptment, in
fact one of the primary means in the history of Christianity,
has been the Book of Common Prayer. What other means to
convey doctrine, offer a pattern of daily and seasonal life,
lead toward conversion, and foster lives of hope and praise,
is so concise or effective? It is no accident that it has been the
framework of new Anglican Churches throughout the world,
and its translation has been the standard by which an indig-
enous Christian idiom has been formed. In this age of viral
worries, an image from virology comes to mind. Within the
cell walls, information is densely encrypted. Quite simply, the
Book of Common Prayer has densely encrypted the faith for
Anglicans, and has proved able to convey that same formation
in many other settings. Its power has been inseparable from
the transformative effect of the translation of Scripture, since
the Prayer Book itself aims to be suffused with Scripture and
so be a means for it to suffuse our prayers.[5] But a question
remains. While the Prayer Book may be the framework for
Anglicans, when it comes to the combustible intensity which

[4] pp. 286, 288.
[5] See Lamin Sanneh's *Translating the Message: the Missionary
Impact on Culture*, (Maryknoll: Orbis, 1989).

is the condition for mission, another factor must be added. For many a parish has used it for years and yet remained sleepy and diffuse. It is a necessary, but not a sufficient, condition for missionary vigour in Anglican history.

Put another way, the Prayer Book provides the encryptment, but mission requires the substructure of the cell which can be introjected into the larger society. It so happens that Martin's prime example of these congenial cells for the conveyance of dense encryptment is actually an Anglican one, namely John Wesley and the Methodists. For Martin, he and his movement are the prime case of adaptation of Christianity to the modern world, the breaking up of the old solidarities, with new pietist cells gathering their strength in the interstices and then spreading forth both in mission and in social reformism. The Brazilian Pentecostals of whom Martin writes are but the next wave of a similar kind of phenomenon; they rank, in Martin's eyes, as Wesley's grandchildren.

What Martin is describing, then, is exemplary of a wider pattern. In short, we can claim that Christian mission tends to exhibit stages in line with what Martin describes in Brazil. We may speak of two stages. First of all, a community must grow up within whose confines the Christian faith and life can be built up with a certain intensity and clarity. Catechesis and liturgy provide this intensity, as do rigorous practices of devotion, or the recounting of martyrologies or the communal endurance of hardship. Once again, these are like the cell wall where information is densely encrypted. Within the walls, density of meaning and intensity of feeling reach a level of combustion by which the Christian community can become a herald of the Gospel, though first it must have this space to itself. So these communities often begin their life tucked away in the interstices of larger societal structures, in the cracks or fissures that Martin describes.

If we may continue our viral trajectory, the second phase involves both introjection of these cells into the larger body politic, and replication of communal cells and practices. With the latter come diffusion of influence and conversion

more widely in society. For example, in the often–maligned
African mission station, this fledgling new Christian life could
be sheltered and intensified in a small space. John Karanja
has described how the first generation of Kenyan converts
would flee to the mission station to avoid an odious planned
marriage, disinheritance, or other social or spiritual confine-
ments.[6] And in those new physical confines they learned the
Christian faith, and so were enabled to return to their villages
for events such as circumcisions, and to witness to their faith
as they declared what their new commitments did and did not
allow them to take part in.

Once the cell has formed itself anew, it must be replicated
and so its influence disseminated in the new situation in ways
multifarious and unpredictable. One may for example, think
of the congregational missionaries in Tahiti, or the Anglicans
in rural India, who as good evangelicals hoped and worked
for the devout conversions of individuals. What they got was
a theocracy on the one hand, and tribal mass conversions on
the other, both cases proving the sense of humour of the Holy
Spirit. To be sure, the intrusion of a new faith in an existing,
solid cultural system is not easy. Introjection is easier where
one finds openings, fissures, spaces. These fissures appear
especially in times of rapid change and extensive social dislocation. In such times the church provides a place to be at home
as well as a large–scale explanation of the world. Its servants,
often people who live between cultures or classes, tribes or
states, can move comfortably in these fissures to bring the
Gospel. If we may return for a moment to the key encryptment
of the Prayer Book, its full missionary potential could not be
seen in the established faith of the Church of England. It is
precisely in the more marginal, stressed, and minority situa-
tions of younger Anglican Churches of the Two-Thirds World
that this potential for propagation through its means can be
seen more clearly.

[6] *Founding an African Church: Kikuyu Anglican Christianity
1900–1945*, (Nairobi: Uzima Press, 1999).

When it comes to evangelism, we often think in terms which are on the one hand too small, and on the other too grand. We think either of individuals sharing the faith – and so they must, or we talk of transforming cultures – and so we Anglicans have hoped to do. But in the history of missions it has been specific, intermediate–sized communities, attaining a certain degree of intensity and so combustibility, which have been the precondition for effective evangelization. In some cases these have been the younger churches, ancient or modern. In other cases various kinds of intermediate institutions become instruments of dense encryptment: religious orders, pietistic *ecclesiolae*, sodalities, cohesive classes of converts like the young courtiers of Buganda, mission societies, Methodist class meetings, Cursillo, or (in the case of Brazil) independent churches. In the Anglican orbit specifically, one may point to the replication of a sodality in the propagation and growth of the Mothers Union (MU), called the 'fifth instrument of unity' by the Archbishop of Canterbury. It was born in the zeal of English evangelicalism, and fostered by Victorian enthusiasm for voluntary societies, but it has gained a great prominence and clout in Africa, where the wife of the bishop heads the MU and serves essentially as a second bishop. Or one may point to a replication that creates something new. An Anglican example of this is the Melanesian Brotherhood, mirroring in its lay vows the monastic tradition of the Anglo–Catholic missionaries. It provided outrigger evangelism and island parish leadership for generations.

In each case the group in question attained within itself the critical mass of belief and piety to make the dispersal possible. In recent years our common life has been characterized by a catechetical, devotional, and ethical thinning out, making missionary energy less likely. So it should be no surprise that talk about the Decade of Evangelism in most places served as a substitute for the real thing. Only with energized density do we find communities with the passion to share an urgent message, and a message in turn that has the distinctiveness to matter as a life–or–death concern to its hearers. Only members of communities with the requisite density can live amidst the contrary commitments of the larger society so as to maintain their bearings and even negotiate appropriated forms of expression of the faith. And, to reiterate, that density has tended to require the kind of doxological, doctrinal, and liturgical encryptment of which the Prayer Book is a prime example. Catechetical seriousness grows out of it, as do mobile and committed subgroups to penetrate and deliver the message.

Let us now apply our theory of dense encryptment to Africa, the epicentre of Anglican mission growth. The story of the growing Church of Anglican East Africa really begins not in Mombasa or Kigali or Kampala but in Clapham and Cambridge, England, with the birth of the Church Missionary Society (CMS). The first and most important thing to note is of course its name: the *Church* Missionary Society, in conscious contrast to their fellow evangelicals in, for example, the London Missionary Society. CMS founders were indeed evangelicals, but they were evangelical churchmen, loyal to the established church even as they decried its moribund nature, and insistent on having often wary bishops on their board. Andrew Walls has stressed that, while evangelicals of the early nineteenth century did indeed think that the Bugandans, to whom the missionaries went, were heathen, they assumed the same thing about most of the proper English gentry in Church of England parishes. And yet the founders of the CMS were adamant about their loyalty to that church.[7]

This proves to be a decisive fact, not only for that era, but for ours as well, not only for those who brought the Gospel, but also for those who received it. A generation ago, an influential book by Charles Hummel about the charismatic movement, was called *Fire in the Fireplace*. Such was the basic assumption of the CMS, that renewal must take place within the confines

[7] 'The Evangelical Revival, the Missionary Movement, and Africa', in *The Missionary Movement in Christian History: Studies in the Transmission of Faith*, ed. Andrew Walls, (Maryknoll: Orbis, 1996, pp. 76–101.

of the church, even as they understood the inevitable tension that this would create. Their theology put conversion at the very center of the Christian life. But Hummel's dedication to the 'fire in the fireplace' – and its concomitant commitment to infant baptism and the Anglican structure oriented to formation of a nation through the gradual effect of common prayer and Bible reading – was bound to co–exist uneasily with the emphasis on the moment of giving one's heart to Jesus. The CMS was made up of evangelicals who deliberately kept themselves under 'Catholic' constraint. It made their ecclesiology messier, and richer too.

The instrument of this churchly Gospel outreach was a voluntary society. This was very much in keeping with the era, which would soon thereafter see a plethora of similar societies. The ecclesiological aptness of the society as instrument did not mean that all went well. The CMS struggled to find Englishmen and women (who soon outnumbered the men) to go on mission, and many of the early missionaries were borrowed Continental Lutherans. When the CMS did find people to go, they died of fever in dauntingly short periods of time. (This was in fact a significant impetus to the idea of a native bishop, the Europeans being incapable of survival long enough for their task.) The converts were few, the demands of the freedmen's town many and seemingly distracting, the only early accomplishment (and in fact the key one) being the mastery of the languages. The traders and first colonialists were decidedly cool toward these religious fanatics troubling the local waters.

Through all these setbacks, CMS was blessed by the remarkable leadership of its first general secretary, Henry Venn, a scion of one of the first families of Anglican evangeli-calism. From the earliest days of CMS and throughout his career spanning the middle of the nineteenth century, Venn was dedicated to the promotion of a mature and independent native Church, with the many risks necessary to avoid dependence. In this he was far ahead of his time. Venn's watchwords 'the euthanasia of the mission' and 'three selves:

self–propagating, self–governing, and self–supporting' became famous in the twentieth century in very different settings, with only partial awareness of the borrowing. But for our purposes it is important to see that he envisioned churches that were in full fellowship with the churches of the missionary guests, of equal maturity and evangelistic responsibility. For all the later problems and inexcusable delays in the attainment, these goals of Venn's set a course that proved decisive, and has made an enormous difference for the eventual vigour of the resulting churches. [8]

The early setbacks were many, but then some remarkable things did happen. Conversion can take place from the bottom up, with individual decisions for Christ as the evangelical missionaries usually hoped, or from the top down, with the decision of the king or chief, a distant reminiscence of medieval Europe and a rarer event. But this is exactly what did occur in Buganda in the 1870s, though it came at a great and famous cost. To the court of the Kabaka came emissaries of Islam, of the Catholic White Fathers, and of the CMS. It is to the fault of the latter two that the listeners could not discern in any way that three religions were not being offered to them, so vitriolic were the mutual critiques of Catholic and Protestant. The key players were the young courtiers, ready for a new spiritual message, excited about their new literacy, urging one another on in their late–night prayer sessions, refusing the sexual advances of the ruling Kabaka, singing hymns to Christ as they made their way to be martyred in the fires of the hill of Namirembe. This was the decisive event, complemented by the martyrdom of missionaries like James Hannington, a CMS missionary. A religious civil war followed, with first the United Christians and then the Anglicans victorious, the latter aided by General Lugard of the British. In this case the colonial military power was drawn reluctantly into the fray by the riveting story of the suffering of the slave

[8] Wilbert Shenk, *Henry Venn: Missionary Statesman*, (Maryknoll: Orbis, 1983), chapter 3.

trade and the resultant outcry in England. In a single stroke the empire of Buganda became Christian, and a majority Anglican. As imperial warriors had once gone out from Buganda, now evangelists fanned out to the client states and beyond, the most famous being the apostle to the pygmies, Apolo Kivebulaya. Of course the huge task of turning a whole society to the Christian way remained; it was aided by a new literate elite and the borrowing of the old clan system for new Christian affiliations.

We are of course telling a much longer tale,[9] yet we are approaching the heart of the matter. The excitement of the first generation of converts gave way to the malaise and discouragement of the second. It seemed that many reverted to pagan practices in times of crisis and stress. Villagers who were fenced from communion because of marital irregularities (often related to polygamy) were more common than not. The transition from mission to church, the handing-over so central to the great Bishop Tucker and to Venn before him, had gone quite sour. And then a second, sudden, remarkable event took place, like a bolt from above. In 1935, the tensions between white members of the CMS Rwanda Mission and the native catechists and leaders were unmistakable. A missionary, Joe Church, met a Bugandan named Nsimbambi and they got to talking about their sense that their spiritual lives were stalled. They were quite frank spiritually, throughout the night admitting openly to one another all their resentments and coming to a state of spiritual reconciliation and invigoration greater than either had ever known. They told others about what had happened, about their putting their sins openly 'in the light,' about their becoming brothers in a new way; and the practice, with the accompanying revival, began to spread, first throughout Buganda, and then outward to Kenya, Tanzania, and Zaire.

What resulted was called the Balokole movement, from the Bugandan word for 'the saved', for that is what those touched

[9] See John V. Taylor, *The Growth of the Church in Buganda: an Attempt at Understanding*, (London: SCM, 1958).

by the Spirit in the movement believed themselves to be. The movement is also called the East African Revival, and it too is a crucial reality to reckon with in understanding African Anglicanism. It was characterized by fellowship meetings in which sins would be confessed and the word of grace heard, in which spiritual accountability and counsel would take place. It had an evangelistic zeal which led to dramatic church growth. It transformed relationships between men and women. (For example in central Tanzania, it was revival men who were first willing to carry water or help with household chores with their wives.) The movement was marked by a certain Puritanism, as the abandonment of smoking and drinking became visible markers of the move from the darkness of the old life to the new light. It retained the strict evangelical refusal to have any truck with any traditional religious practice, though it took over the healing and purifying functions therein. It was not for the most part Pentecostal in the sense we think of today. On the negative side of the ledger, it could evince a certain judgmentalism, as Balokole would in the early days sit in trees outside churches and shout out the secret sins of parishioners as they exited the services.[10]

The significance of the revival was this: by its means East African Anglicans found a way to be evangelical and Anglican in a uniquely East African way. The revival's origin and its leadership were totally East African. Whatever inculturation should mean, this was a legitimate form for that process in East Africa. For our present purposes, it should be noted that this 'inculturated' Church, in the subsequent years, showed little interest in innovation liturgically. They believed that the missionaries, men and women of prayer and self-sacrifice, had brought them the Gospel in a sacred vessel, and that their task was to hand it on faithfully. This sense of handing on the Prayer Book, in a way analogous to their ancestors handed on tradition, is precisely what was indigenized. This did not mean that they were not innovators: social forms adapted to clan

[10] See Max Warren, *Revival: An Inquiry*, (London: SCM, 1954).

particularities, original music, styles of preaching adapted to African emphases, etc. These all took place, as it were, around the structure of the Prayer Book. The continuity of the Prayer Book was a key means of this, not an obstacle, as a more simplistic read of liturgical inculturation might suppose.

An Anglican revivalism with small group accountability and perfectionist tendencies? What is the precedent for that? There is no evidence that the revival's originators knew anything of the theology or spirituality of John Wesley, but the parallels are uncanny. And the danger was identical as well, for the revival took place in the environment of Uganda and Kenya, both of which had many break-away African independent churches. The risk was that the revival would split off from Anglicanism, just as the Methodists had two centuries earlier. In fact there were some minor defections. But for the most part they remained in the Anglican fold, in no small part because of some judicious CMS bishops in the 1940s who were willing to compromise and so avert a crisis provoked by protest against what was seen as the theological modernism at the theological college. To this fact, fraught with consequences for African and global Anglicanism, we shall return shortly.

There is a key fact to note: the similarity between the parent CMS and the progeny, the revival, insofar as it was a movement and a sodality distinct from but loyally within the episcopal structures of the church. As significant as what the revival did, what was more important was what happened afterwards. In a revival the worry is always what in Swahili is called 'kupoa', cooling. Inevitably the revival did cool, though it is still a tangible force with roughly the same shape as in its beginning. Of equal significance, it was able to make the transition to established leadership, to providing most of the bishops in the East African churches. It was able to institutionalize its revivalist influence. The note on holiness, the zeal for evangelism, and the stress on decisive conversion have been conveyed to the church as a whole, while its theological shortcomings have endured as well. And in East Africa these qualities have a close relationship to the uneven but continual and at times dramatic growth of the churches.

Yet more surprising has been what might be called intra-Anglican ecumenism. Tanzania is unique in having a province with churches founded by the CMS and by the Universities' Mission to Central Africa (UMCA), the very Anglo–Catholic society founded in the mid-nineteenth century in the wake of publicity around the work of David Livingstone. The highest and lowest of Anglicans worship together in a single province, and recent years have seen continually closer cooperation. This too can be traced in part to the ecclesial loyalty and stalwart Anglican identity which was part of the Balokole identity along with its revival emphases. These qualities of loyalty and identity have held firm in spite of church environments throughout most of East Africa and Nigeria that are enormously fragmenting and fissiparous. New independent churches spring up like flora in the rainy season. These qualities are not irrelevant to the present stress within the Anglican Communion.

What, then, are the lessons from our general theory of dense encryptment and its Anglican exemplar, the CMS and the East African revival? What do we learn about mission effectiveness and Anglican identity? Three lessons apply directly to the situation of our churches in the West today, the first doctrinal, the second structural, and the third practical. This is a moment when we need to think through what it truly means to be a church catholic: a church that is global, worldwide. Only with a strong sense of this credal affirmation can we make good use of terms like 'incarnational' or 'contextual'. The Balokole had strong views, and so may we, whether leaning to the liberal or conservative side; but the Balokole were ecclesially constrained. As Anglicans, they understood themselves to be 'fire in the fireplace' even when it seemed costly to them. The catholic cause has in many ways won the day (for example, in the near universality of Sunday Eucharist). Now we are challenged to accept the conciliar and constraining implications of catholicity as well. Philip Turner and Ephraim

Radner's eloquent book *The Fate of Communion*[11] makes the case that this conciliar and catholic dimension is integral to what it means to be an Anglican.

Following closely is a second point about the importance of societies, what the Roman Catholics call 'sodalities'. They do not really fit, but reside uneasily in the interstices of the church. That is their strength. Healing groups, social action committees, and charismatic cells are sometimes messy and problematic. They are also sources of new life and missionary vigour. We need to find ways to encourage and guide them, as did those wise though harried bishops in Uganda in the 1940s. We Anglicans are not alone in having renewal groups and mission societies, but the spaciousness of our comprehensive ethos and synodical structure makes their flourishing possible. We need to encourage the fires lit in the fireplace.

Third and finally, we need to do an inventory of our 'dense encryptment' rating. For that is the best indicator of initiative and fervour in mission. The original goal of the Book of Common Prayer, and its continued potential, is for just such encryptment in the life of a parish. Think, for example, of the theology of atonement and self-sacrifice packed into the Eucharistic Prayers of the Book of Common Prayer. Much has been written about a theology of baptism in recent years, but a corollary must be the renewal of rigorous practices of catechesis, of teaching and forming new or newly inter-ested Christians. Authors like William Abraham and Robert Webber[12] have proposed that catechesis is at the heart of an evangelism friendly to a tradition like ours. How much do we expect of adult baptizands? How effective are we at leading them into a Bible study? How well do we use episodic training like camp, Cursillo, and women's or men's retreats? How well

---

[11] Grand Rapids: Eerdmans, 2006.
[12] William Abraham, *The Logic of Evangelism* (Grand Rapids: Eerdmans, 1989); Robert Webber, *Ancient-Future Evangelism: Making Your Church a Faith-Forming Community*, (Grand Rapids: Baker, 2003).

do we reiterate that such intense formative experiences of the faith should serve the building up of the whole?

Our prayer is that this decade, as every decade, will be one of evangelism. Our hope is that such evangelism will indeed be sensitive to context, and will follow in the tracks of what God is doing in the world. But as Anglicans, we will achieve these goods best, and be truest to ourselves, as we are catholically constrained, enlivened in cells and societies, and densely formed in teaching, all for the realization the Father's will and reign on earth.

Inspiring Young People with the Book of Common Prayer

Fredrik Arvidsson

The Revd Fredrik Arvidsson was born in Stockholm, and arrived in England at the age of twelve. He went on to attend Agricultural College and, after a period in farming, trained for the ordained ministry at Regents and Chichester Theological Colleges. Having served in inner-city Portsmouth and then in a country parish, he took up his first incumbency in the Canterbury Diocese, where he was for a time Chairman of the Diocesan Liturgical Committee.

He is currently Senior Chaplain at The King's School, Canterbury where he teaches Religious Studies and Personal, Social and Health Education, and is an Honorary Minor Canon of Canterbury Cathedral.

He was previously a Trustee of the Prayer Book Society and is currently its Youth Officer. In his spare time he keeps chickens, rides and shoots. He is married to Amelia and they have three children.

As the Senior Chaplain of a public school said to be the oldest in England – an institution dating back to 597 AD – I have inherited a very rich and wonderful tradition working within the beautiful surroundings of Canterbury Cathedral. The King's School has grown up over an extraordinary length of time; traditional values are at its heart, but we live in a fast-moving and ever-changing society and are acutely aware that we must not only achieve success whilst our pupils are at school, but also equip them for the future. Indeed, although our pupils leave us after five years, our aim is that King's will never leave them.

The Archbishop of Canterbury, who is a great friend of and frequent visitor to the school, recently Confirmed 85 of our pupils at a Prayer Book Service in the Cathedral. During the service, he said that 'The Book of Common Prayer remains a deeply valuable spiritual resource for people of all ages. It offers a wealth of words and images to deepen prayer and enrich imagination, and I am delighted to see younger people having the opportunity of experiencing this richness'. The Confirmation was attended by 30 newly consecrated bishops from around the world, who were staying for ten days as guests of the Archbishop. Subsequently, I was delighted to receive a letter from the Rt Revd Michael Hawkins, Bishop of Saskatchewan, Canada, which he has given me permission to reproduce:

Dear Fredrik,
Thank you so much for your tour of the school and showing us the grave of St. Augustine etc ... ... The Sunday Confirmation service was a delight for me and now when I get ridiculed for using the Prayer Book especially for Baptism and Confirmation, I will recall last Sunday. The Service was the highlight of my stay in Canterbury. God Bless you.
+Michael

I have lost count the number of former pupils wanting to come back to our Prayer Book services and asking me to reserve them front row seats. I am not lost in a wonderful Trollopian world walking around in my cassock and listening to Elgar and Vaughan Williams (although at times I do these things). My music collection also includes Lady Gaga and Chet Baker; this is not because I am trying to stay young and be trendy with my pupils, but because I actually like it! I have three teenage children of my own and I am in charge of teaching and planning of the Personal, Social and Health Education syllabus ('sex and drugs' as young people call it) for the Upper School, so I *do* live in the 'real world'.

When I first arrived at King's ten years ago, I received the standard letter from the local Bishop stating his terms and conditions for his visits to the parishes or the schools regarding baptism and confirmation services. It talked about the new Common Worship and had all the typical 'sales talk' about the exciting new liturgy. At the end of his Episcopal letter, there was a brief line saying that some might still want to use the Book of Common Prayer. I organised and prepared my group of 80 candidates and sent the service that I had put together from the Prayer Book Confirmation and Communion rites to his Domestic Chaplain for his perusal. I went to the Bishop's office to see him to talk about the great day, when 80 youngsters entered the church in full membership; I anticipated a pat on the back; I thought he might greet me with a smile and a 'well done, what a superb number you have this year', but I was to be sadly disappointed. 'Fredrik,' he said in a rather disapproving tone of voice, 'What is this? The Book of Common Prayer? Are you mad?' I replied, puzzled, that he had said in his letter that we could choose the Book of Common Prayer service. He replied 'It's only there because it is part of the Church's Traditional liturgy; I didn't think people would choose the ruddy thing. I will be grinding my teeth during the peace, knowing very well there is none.' As I left, I pondered that what was good enough for the Supreme Governor of the Church of England ought to be good enough for the bishop. I had just picked up a Confirmation service sheet from St. James's Palace.

There are so many ways of using Cranmer's wonderful liturgy with young people and making it relevant and appealing to them without changing a word of it. I have often asked the pupils if they would like to look at other modes of worship, but such suggestions of change make them uncomfortable. Amid their fast-paced world of computers, smartphones, social networking sites and satellite television, they are seeking some stability. They need and want a sense of belonging and mystery which they find in the Book of Common Prayer. Young people are asking for, and need, dignified worship – but it needs to be done well and with an engaging sermon. It is sometimes said that younger people find the Prayer Book inaccessible. This may initially be true for some, but if it is taught properly and with love, feeling, meaning and a sense of belonging, it does not take long to comprehend – it is not difficult to grasp that 'manifold' is not only a part of a car! The Prayer Book works as long as the clergy are willing and excited about using it, and are not looking over their shoulders worrying that too much enthusiasm for the Book of Common Prayer might not meet with the approval of the church hierarchy.

When reaching out to young people, the important thing is to present them with a liturgy and sermon with music that is dignified and does not patronize them. As the Revd Michel Green said in relation to God: 'He is not the pal across the street to whom we chat while we're chewing gum with our hands in our pockets'. We are dealing with an awesome God who works in all our lives. There is a fitting sense of awe before God in the Prayer Book, and awe is one of the things which is most notably lacking in contemporary Christianity; it is also very lacking in the banalities of some sermons and in certain elements of Common Worship.

At the same time, the Book of Common Prayer can easily be used with times of extemporary prayer, with drama, with modern music, with choruses and at times even using an overhead projector (this works very well with the very young at the Prep. school). All this can be done with some imagination and prayer and without confusing worship with entertainment – a danger that too many churches fall into in a desire to keep young people in their congregations.

But we must be very sure that we do not cling to the Prayer Book for the wrong reasons. The value of the Book of Common Prayer is not only in its language. Nor must we cling to the Prayer Book out of blind conservatism. The Christian faith, like many young people, is radical in many ways; but so is the Book of Common Prayer. We must not allow ourselves to be misrepresented simply as reactionaries who do not like change. There is so much in that small volume which can nurture the young here in the twenty-first century, almost every word of which comes from Scripture.

There is another very good reason for using the Book of Common Prayer with young people and helping them to learn to treasure it. I believe that a significant part of my ministry is to encourage them to love and cherish the Church of England, and to join a parish as they leave school and enter university. For them to leave my pastoral care and have no understanding of the background or foundations of Anglicanism would be a matter of great regret. I do not want to hear any of my former pupils saying, as some young people do, 'Fancy you being an Anglican! I used to be an Anglican too, before I became a Christian'. I do not want any of them to tell me that he or she is now an ex-Anglican who has left the church because it seems to stand for so little. The Book of Common Prayer is one of the doctrinal norms of Anglicanism and it must not be lost. The doctrine of the Prayer Book reflects the catholic faith of the Established Church in England If anyone asks what the Anglican Church believes, there has always been an answer. It may not be the kind of clarity which some are looking for, but nonetheless it is a perfectly clear answer. The beliefs of the Anglican Church can be found in the Book of Common Prayer.

The Book of Common Prayer is our guide to worship and devotion used in our daily relationship with God. The Prayer Book can be complicated even for lifelong Anglicans and can seem even more bewildering for visitors and newcomers. Nevertheless, I have found that, working in a school with young people, once they become familiar with the pages of this treasure house they come to love the book and its liturgy. It may have been compiled over 450 years ago and revised a little more than a century later, but if it is used today then it becomes a *modern* liturgy used by *modern* people.

Keep using it, the modern liturgy of the Book of Common Prayer!

Postscript

A Very Present Help in Trouble

Terry Waite

Terry Waite CBE is an Anglican Layman who has spent much of his life in the service of the Church both in the UK and throughout the world. In recent years he became a full member of the Society of Friends (Quakers) but continues to remain loyal to his Anglican roots.

When working for the late Archbishop of Canterbury, Robert Runcie, he negotiated the release of many hostages. In 1987, he was himself captured in Beirut and spent almost five years in captivity, most of which time was spent in strict solitary confinement. It was during this time that he especially grew to value the language of the Book of Common Prayer which, unconsciously, he had committed to memory through regular usage across life. The harmony of language enabled him to maintain a degree of harmony within during difficult days.

Today he continues to be active in many humanitarian endeavours. He is a joint founder of Hostage UK and Y Care International, and took over from Robert Runcie as President of Emmaus UK, an organisation for the homeless.

He is married with four children and three grandchildren

To be in strict solitary confinement for many years can be both a depressing and a debilitating experience. For almost five years I was kept alone in a room with no natural light. My hands and feet were shackled to a wall and I was not allowed books or any contact whatsoever with the outside world. During those long days I saw my skin turn white because of the lack of daylight. I lost muscle tone as there was no opportunity for exercise. My beard grew long and white and I recollect thinking that I was growing old before my time. Most people manage to grow old with reasonable grace but it seemed as though even this was denied me. As I saw my physical body begin to deteriorate rather more quickly than I hoped for I wondered if I might begin to disintegrate within. Would I fall apart mentally and spiritually? As a child I had read of individuals who had been kept for prolonged periods in solitary confinement and it seemed that the majority, on release, had lost their power of speech or had sunk into mental illness. Naturally, I wondered if this result was an inevitable consequence of extreme solitude.

I quickly realised that it was necessary to find a way of dealing with this unusual circumstance. Much of my life had been spent in a very active way. I had been a constant traveller and was always meeting new people and visiting new places. Now, all that came to an abrupt halt and I was confined in a small room in Beirut.

It took me only a short time to recognise that whilst this experience was far from pleasant it need not be totally disastrous. Even in this bleak outpost there were new opportunities of which to seize hold. Now was the time to take an inner journey, to go more deeply into understanding the roots of my identity and hopefully work towards a greater inner harmony. I fully recognised that this could be a dangerous journey, for when I encountered the dark side of my personality I might fall into a depression from which there might be no escape. I realised that one needed to take the view that one was simply a normal human being with both positive and negative aspects of character, and rather than work for one to subdue the other one needed to work for a greater inner harmony.

I further recognised that in order to take this journey I needed guidelines onto which I could hold as I struggled along the interior pathway. I began where most such journeys begin and that is back in memory to the very earliest recollections of my life on earth. There were people and events that had imprinted themselves on my mind. Over the years the memories may have become distorted or even false but the pictures had been formed and I could look at them. As I looked at the pictures of my life I began to write in my head in an attempt to give some coherent narrative to the stream of recollections that were being brought into consciousness. It was at this point that I began to appreciate more fully the importance of good language. As a child I had been encouraged – no, commanded – to learn certain scripts by rote. They had lodged in the recesses of my mind and I could now retrieve them. The importance of this experience was that good language, like good music, has the capacity to breathe a certain harmony into the soul and throughout this experience I was seeking inner harmony and attempting not to disintegrate within. I consciously refused to engage in extempore prayer for I believed that if I did so I would simply fall into pleading with God to get me out of this experience and thus demoralise myself. Rather, I fell back on that which I had unconsciously assimilated as a child.

From the very earliest days I had been an attender at Church, first at Sunday School and later as a chorister. In those days, through frequent repetition virtually the whole of the services of the Church contained in the Book of Common Prayer and many of the Psalms had, unconsciously, been committed to memory. The lovely collect, 'Lighten our darkness we beseech thee O Lord; and by thy great mercy defend us from all the perils and dangers of this night ...' takes on a deep significance when one is afraid and sitting in darkness. Within the structure of the language there is harmony and the soul longs to be nourished by harmony.

I had no Prayer Book by my side but each morning I could recite to myself the Service of Holy Communion and communicate myself with a small piece of bread saved from my meagre breakfast and water taken from my beaker. I consoled myself by thinking that as I sat alone I was in fact joining with thousands of people across the world who were reciting the same words as I was.

The language and structure of the Prayer Book gave me, in a time of crisis, the necessary supports to continue on the journey toward greater wholeness, a journey that still continues of course.

I know full well that language is fluid and that we must not become fixed in archaic expressions. I also know that we have a need for language that can inspire and nourish. In Lambeth Palace, before I was captured, I would sometimes go and sit in the small room by the chapel where it is said that parts of the Prayer Book were written. Little did I know then that it would be one of the means to my survival.

It is my view that in an understandable desire to communicate to a wider group of worshippers some liturgical revisers have failed to appreciate the importance of language that has significance, not only because of its frequent use across the years, but also because of its symbolic value. Symbols compress a wealth and depth of meaning which is intuitively received and interpreted by the recipient. This process takes place at a level different from cognitive understanding. The depth of meaning inherent within the symbol speaks directly to the soul and thus the soul is nourished and sustained.

I was always a regular attender at the early morning said Communion Service where the Book of Common Prayer was used. One might remain sitting or kneeling throughout. One was conscious of being a participant in the whole mystery of the service and the contemplative experience was not disturbed by being requested to stand, sit or make frequent verbal responses. A similar experience might be found within the context of Orthodox worship where an individual worshipper may be alone with his or her own devotions but also caught up with the total action of the service.

Today, or so it seems to me, the contemplative aspect within Anglican worship has been somewhat lost in the desire to encourage participation by bodily action and verbal response. Stand, sit, greet your neighbour are all laudable actions in themselves but for me they do not contribute to that deep level of contemplative communication for which the soul longs.

As I mentioned earlier in this essay, during the years of separation from normal life and worship I could call upon language and structure that I has assimilated from my very earliest days. Such supports will not necessarily be available to a generation brought up with extemporary language and a variety of services across a Church which is no longer united by the use of a common language of worship. One of the intentions of the compilers was to establish such a common language and to establish unity through language. According to the Book of Common Prayer such unity was not expected to be rigidly enforced, however.

As a choirboy endlessly leafing through the book during many a long and incomprehensible sermon one sentence frequently caught my eye: 'It hath been the wisdom of the Church of England, ever since the first compiling of her publick Liturgy, to keep the mean between the two extremes, of too much stiffness in refusing, and of too much easiness in admitting any variation from it'. That one sentence captures in a nutshell the essence of Anglicanism. It speaks to me of balance and harmony found within the language of the book. That was exactly what I needed during the years spent alone and that was what the Book of Common Prayer provided.

Although I remain an Anglican, in recent years I have also become a full member of the Society of Friends, or the Quakers are they as more commonly known. There are a number of reasons for my joining the Friends but one important reason for me is that they understand the importance and value of silence in worship. I continue to attend liturgical worship but find that there I have a need to move beyond that into a corporate contemplative experience such as may be found in Quaker worship. The Book of Common Prayer gave me guidelines and a structure which enabled me to find my bearings and to move forward into a deeper exploration of the great mystery that is God.

It was John Henry Newman who put words into the mouth of one of his characters in the novel *Loss and Gain* to which I find I can heartily subscribe and with which I will conclude this brief contribution: 'I value the Prayer Book as you cannot do for I have known what it is to one in affliction. May it be long before you know it in a similar way; but if affliction comes on you, depend on it. All these new Fancies and fashions will vanish from you like the wind, and the good old Prayer Book alone will stand you in any stead'.

Afterword

Will the events of the 350th anniversary year of the publication of the 1662 Book of Common Prayer prove to be a prolonged funeral service, or could the celebrations assist in confirming the place of the Prayer Book as part of the living tradition of the English Church?

There are certainly those who regard the BCP as a museum piece.

In 2011 there was a fascinating example of an antipathy to the Prayer Book in the reaction to the choice of the traditional liturgy (as revised in 1928) for the Royal Wedding in Westminster Abbey. In the acres of commentary in the secular press there was no criticism of the couple's decision to use the traditional language form of the service. A week later, however, the Church Times published letters from clergy deploring the 'archaic order' and expressing exasperation that 'the language of the liturgy remained buried in the past' and that 'once again the opportunity to present the church in a more up-to-date way was missed'.

In the following week's edition of the paper, another clergyman wrote to point out that the three who had decried the 'stuffy service' were born respectively in 1960, 1951 and 1937. The royal couple who had chosen the service were both born in 1982, and the author of the letter suggested that we should allow the young people their voice in church since 'it would appear that nothing dates so rapidly as yesterday's modernity'.

I have no desire to promote a cult of quaintness, but the power of the Prayer Book to connect with many of those who find the ordinary diet of the church banal should not be ignored.

Members of the Church of England who cherish the
Prayer Book tradition do, of course, owe a great deal to
Archbishop Cranmer whose contribution has been discussed
in this book. But we are not Cranmerians in the sense that
Lutherans and Calvinists look to a master theologian for
their inspiration. Much that we cherish, including Choral
Evensong, would not necessarily be approved by the
Archbishop; but we honour him and we celebrate his contri-
bution to the spiritual life of this and of every nation which
worships in English.

In the sixteenth century, English was being shaped to
encompass the highest themes. It could have developed in
two ways. One way would have led to the pompous and
convoluted style favoured by some humanist scholars, with an
excessive dependence on the classical languages.

The other path, favoured by men like Cranmer's friend
Sir John Cheke, would have seen a consistent preference for
Anglo-Saxon derivations over Latin and Greek. He proposed,
for example, that instead of resurrection we should speak of
'gainrising'; crucified would have been 'crossed' and proselyte
– 'freshman'.

The Prayer Book played a key role in deciding what was
good English. We can thank God that it was composed by
Thomas Cranmer, who had an ear for formal prose: for its
sonorities and structure.

But there is much more. Just before Christmas, I went to
take the sacrament to someone who was putting up a brave
fight against cancer and who has since died. I used the Prayer
Book Communion Service which he had not heard for many
years. The power of the liturgy – its 'in your face quality' – did
not alienate him at such a grave moment but rather liberated
him to face the deep and simple questions that somehow elude
us in the coded speech of more modern times. The liturgy
enabled him to 'lift up his heart' and left him more joyful and
positive.

In particular, it was such a relief not to lurch into the indic-
ative mood of 'the Lord is here' – that proprietorial sentence

which so jars on the ears of those who have a lively sense, in prayer, of the immensity in our midst.

The proper mood in worship is adorative and implorative. True, a generation that has been outrageously flattered and has a very good opinion of itself (until reminded by affliction of its own creaturely existence) has found the liturgy of the Prayer Book insufficiently affirming. But that is precisely why it is vital that the BCP is not relegated to some liturgical museum, because it preserves in its DNA things that are virtually unsayable now but which, with the revolution of the times, will come into focus once again.

The Prayer Book system embodies the ethos of our Church which is founded on scripture, interpreted by tradition, which is not only articulated by the catholic creeds (perhaps more commonly used in the Prayer Book liturgies than in any other liturgical regime) but which is also expressed by the spirit-filled continuity of life in the Church and the ways in which we have sought together to respond to the demands of successive generations.

Tradition for us is not 'traditionalism' – the obstinate adherence to morés of the day before yesterday – but rather the spirit-filled continuity of the Church's life and her response to contemporary challenge, always under the supreme judgment and inspiration of scripture.

Cranmer himself was a renovator rather than an innovator, and composed our Prayer Book from scripture and the deposits laid down in the course of the history of the Church. He understood that God said, 'Behold I make all things new' and that He did not say, 'Behold I make all new things'.

The Prayer Book offers a simple and moderate system for a whole life from baptism to last rites and seeks, in its rubrics and ceremonies, to embrace the whole person and not merely the cerebellum.

Now is all this at an end? Is the Prayer Book a dead book, a museum piece? I think we certainly need to tell the story with more confidence, as a system which transforms lives and translates doctrines and ethics into living ethos. The formation offered by the Prayer Book is life-long, and demands – and expects – a great deal from those who use it. While we live, we must help new generations who grow sick of perpetual carnival with no ensuing Lent to appreciate that there is, in the Prayer Book system, a sure though not flashy way to Transfiguration, and to Heaven beyond.

+Richard Londin:

Acknowledgements

In addition to the contributors, particular recognition is due to the Revd Canon Eric Woods, who was the progenitor of the idea for this book, and without whose considerable initial efforts it would not have come into being.

I should also like to offer my grateful thanks to the Revd George Westhaver and to John Scrivener for helpful advice and suggestions; and to my Commissioning Editor, Caroline Chartres, for her guidance and patience.